Frances Hodgson
◆ Burnett ◆

Frances Hodgson
◆ Burnett ◆

Beyond the Secret Garden

Angelica Shirley Carpenter
and Jean Shirley

Lerner Publications Company • Minneapolis

Page 1: Frances' favorite photo from her later years. She disliked most pictures of herself.
Page 2: Frances in her late 30s, at the time she won a famous British lawsuit.

This edition of this book is available in two bindings:
Library binding by Lerner Publications Company
Soft cover by First Avenue Editions
241 First Avenue North
Minneapolis, Minnesota 55401

Text permissions acknowledgments and source notes appear
on pages 127 and 128, which are an extension of the copyright page.

Library of Congress Cataloging-in-Publication Data

Carpenter, Angelica Shirley.
    Frances Hodgson Burnett : beyond the secret garden / Angelica
Shirley Carpenter and Jean Shirley.
        p.   cm.
    Contents: Includes bibliographical references.
    Summary: A biography of the author of many popular novels and
plays for both adults and children, including the well-known "Little
Lord Fauntleroy" and "The Secret Garden."
    ISBN 0-8225-4905-0 (lib. bdg.)
    ISBN 0-8225-9610-5 (pbk.)
    1. Burnett, Frances Hodgson, 1849-1924—Juvenile literature.
2. Authors, American—19th century—Biography—Juvenile literature.
3. Children's stories, American—History and criticism—Juvenile
literature. [1. Burnett, Frances Hodgson, 1849-1924. 2. Authors,
American.] I. Shirley, Jean. II. Title.
PS1216.C37   1990
813'.4—dc20   90-32088
                                                         CIP
                                                          AC

Manufactured in the United States of America

3   4   5   6   7   8   9   10   99   98   97   96   95   94   93   92

Note to Readers

Frances Hodgson Burnett was a best-selling author and an international celebrity. Her life spanned the time from the Civil War to silent movies. She was born in England and later became a United States citizen. Her book *Little Lord Fauntleroy* started a worldwide fashion craze in 1886. Now she is known best for *The Secret Garden*.

In 1883, Burnett published her autobiography, *The One I Knew the Best of All*. For that book, she wrote conversations based on her childhood memories. We have used her dialogue in chapters one and two. All quotations in this book come from written sources. See pages 123 and 127 for details.

This book is dedicated with love to
LaVerne Ostendorf

Contents

1 *Manchester, England, 1849-1865* 9

2 *Tennessee: The Dryad Days, 1865-1868* . . 19

3 *Knoxville to Paris, 1869-1875* 29

4 *Paris to Washington, 1875-1884* 39

5 *Little Lord Fauntleroy, 1884-1886* 49

6 *Sara Crewe, 1886-1887* 55

7 *Frances Changes the Law, 1887-1888* 61

8 *The Loss of a Son, 1889-1890* 69

9 *Life after Death, 1891-1892* 79

10 *Rumors, 1892-1898* 85

11 *The Walled Garden, 1898-1907* 93

12 *The Secret Garden, 1908-1910* 103

13 *The End of the Story, 1910-1924* 107

14 *Epilogue* 117

Major Sources for This Book 122

For Further Reading 122

Index 124

Maps appear on pages 17 and 31.

Fannie Hodgson, as she was known then, at age 22. This photo was taken at the time of her first visit to New York. She had red hair, blue eyes, and fair skin.

✦ ONE ✦

Manchester, England

1849-1865

Frances could hardly wait to find out what was behind the green door. For years she had wondered. The door was set in a high brick wall. It was too tall to climb—she had tried. Inside was the back yard of a large, vacant house. For years the little girl had longed to explore that yard. Always before, the door had been locked. Now, said the neighborhood gossip, the house was to be torn down. Now she could open the green door.

Frances turned the knob and pushed the door open. Inside was a dreary scene—piles of dirt and rubbish, covered with cinders. Weeds were the only plants. But Frances was not disappointed. Placing her high-buttoned shoes carefully, she made her way into the yard. Since Frances was English, she called it a *garden* instead of a *yard*.

Stooping to touch a small, prickly leaf, she felt grateful

to the weeds for growing in the hard earth. In some spots they covered the ground entirely. "Suppose they were roses and pansies and lilies and violets," she said. "How beautiful it would be!" She walked around, pretending. Her cheeks were flushed, and her red curls glowed in the gray light.

"You *are* roses!" she said to a clump of weeds. She pointed her plump finger. "You *are* violets and lilies—and hyacinths and daffodils and snow drops! You *are*!" Soon the rubbish heaps became fountains, and a ditch turned into a castle moat. The poor old garden bloomed that afternoon as it never had before.

Fifty years later, in 1911, a grown-up Frances wrote a book about another little girl who opened a door into a secret garden. By then, Frances was one of the best-selling authors in the world. Many of her stories had the theme "rags to riches," and so did her real life. She overcame great poverty and earned a fortune with her pen. She said writing was hard work.

Frances described Manchester as a city of factories "over which the huge chimneys towered and rolled their volume of black smoke."

Frances' birthplace, No. 385 Cheetham Hill Road, Manchester, Lancashire, England

Frances was born in the industrial city of Manchester, in the county of Lancashire, England, on November 24, 1849. Her full name was Frances Eliza Hodgson, but everyone called her Fannie.

The Hodgsons lived comfortably in that bustling, filthy city. The air smelled like smoke. Buildings and streets were covered with "smuts" that fell from factory chimneys. Manchester was the center of the world's cotton textile business. Factories called mills made cotton into thread and cloth. Most of the city's residents, rich and poor, made their money from cotton.

Frances' father, Edwin Hodgson, owned a profitable store. Hodgson's General Furnishing Business sold silver tea sets, chandeliers, and hardware. In 1852 when Frances was two, Mr. Hodgson moved his growing family to a seven-room house on the outskirts of town.

He died of a stroke when Frances was only three. Her brothers, John and Herbert, were six and seven. Her little sister, Edith, was two. Frances' mother, Eliza Boond Hodgson, gave birth to another daughter soon after her husband's death. She named the baby Edwina, after her husband.

Although Mrs. Hodgson had two servants to help with the children, she had very little money. She decided to run the store herself, even though middle-class women did not usually work outside the home. She did her best, but she was inexperienced, and Manchester was entering a period of hard times. Business dropped off.

Even though the family had less money than before, they did not consider themselves poor. Schooling cost money, but somehow Mrs. Hodgson saved enough to send all five children to school.

When Frances was five, Mrs. Hodgson moved her family to a poorer neighborhood, Islington Square, their home for the next nine years. The houses on the Square were large and run-down. Once they had been elegant.

Factory workers lived on the streets surrounding the Square. There, houses and even basements were subdivided so that many families lived in each one. Shacks and shanties filled the yards. The streets were open sewers, and pigs rooted through piles of garbage. The "Street children" worked in the factories with their parents for pitiful wages. Some had no shoes and walked barefoot in the snow. Nearly half the children in Manchester died before they reached the age of five.

"Square children" were not allowed to play with "Street

children," but they did anyway. Poor people were not nice, Frances was taught. They did not speak proper English. But Frances loved the Street children and the way they talked. She learned to imitate their Lancashire dialect. She watched the factory workers from her window, and made up stories about their lives.

Frances had always liked stories. She learned to read at the age of three. Soon she could read the Bible, and history books and romances. She preferred books with exciting plots, like *Uncle Tom's Cabin* by Harriet Beecher Stowe, or novels by Charles Dickens and James Fenimore Cooper. She wanted adventure!

Alone in the nursery, she made up thrilling stories to act out with her doll. Her doll was always the heroine, beautiful and strong, who won in the end. Frances herself played all the other roles. She became the hero, the villain, the pirates, the king, the Indian warriors, or whoever was needed.

Riding on the arms of the green nursery sofa, she and her doll chased each other through forests and across plains. They spoke in whispers so Frances' brothers could not hear. "Slightly cracked," the boys would say.

Frances and her sister Edith attended the Miss Hadfields' school in Islington Square. Two or three afternoons each week, the schoolgirls did "fancy-work" — embroidery, crocheting, or sewing. They took turns reading aloud.

One day Frances told a story she made up herself, about a beautiful heroine named Edith Somerville. Edith had violet eyes and "long thick heavy curls which fell almost to her knee." Like Frances' doll, Edith survived many spectacular adventures. She always defeated the villain and won true love. Her story was so popular that Frances had to continue it for weeks. Soon she was the only storyteller allowed.

Next, Frances began writing at home. At about the age of 10, she wrote:

ALONE.
Alone—alone! The wind shrieks "Alone!"
And mocks my lonely sorrow,
"Alone—alone!" the trees seem to moan,
"For thee there's no bright to-morrow."

The next five verses of the poem (now lost) were humorous, about a bachelor who could not take care of himself. Later, Frances read the poem to her mother. It made them both laugh.

"Do you think it's funny?" Frances asked.

"Funny!" exclaimed Mrs. Hodgson. "Oh it is *very* funny!

Artist Reginald Birch drew this picture of Frances and her mother for Frances' autobiography.

Where did you find it? Did you copy it out of one of the periodicals?"

Frances became quite red. "I—didn't get it from anywhere." She hesitated. "I thought you knew. I—I wrote it myself."

Mrs. Hodgson reached for her daughter's exercise book. She studied the poem in amazement. That a child could do such a thing! She decided that Frances was very clever. She was proud of Frances' writing.

Herbert and John were not. "I say!" they would proclaim, "she's writing a three-volumed novel. The heroine has golden hair that trails on the ground."

But Frances was used to them. "You cannot stop boys," she wrote later, "unless you Murder them... If you call names and stamp your feet they will tease you more; if you burst out crying they will laugh and say that it is always the way with girls, so upon the whole it seems better to try not to *look* in a rage and keep your fury inside the little bodice of your frock." She wrote in secret and hid her work from the boys.

By the time Frances was a teenager, the Hodgsons had almost no money coming in. Frances wrote her stories on slates and on old grocery lists—new paper was too expensive. Her brothers were old enough now to work, but no jobs were available. Times were hard in Manchester because of the Civil War in America.

For years Frances had heard about the war in the United States. The North was fighting the South, and the South was losing. Herbert and John told stories of terrible battles. Each day the news was worse, and people prayed for the war to end.

While the fighting continued, no cotton could be grown in the South. England lost its main supply of raw material.

No cotton meant no work in the textile mills, which closed, one by one. The owners lost their money, and without jobs, the workers began to starve. Mrs. Hodgson was forced to sell the store. What would they do when the money ran out?

Near the end of the war in 1864, Mrs. Hodgson received a letter from her brother in Tennessee. He invited her to bring the children to Knoxville. He offered to help find jobs for the boys.

America! Frances knew it only from books. There were beautiful magnolia trees and noble Indians. The street called Broadway was a half-mile wide, with buildings that made Buckingham Palace look small. America meant adventure!

During the cotton shortage, charitable groups started soup kitchens in Manchester, but people still starved. In 1862, more than 310,000 of the city's mill workers were unemployed.

Europe before World War I, during the time Frances lived and visited there.

Although Frances would cross the ocean 32 more times in her life, it seemed likely in 1865 that she would never see England again. The Hodgsons felt as if they were saying goodbye forever. A large party of aunts, cousins, and friends traveled with them on the train to Liverpool. There the

Hodgsons would board a steamship to cross the ocean. The whole party stayed one night in a hotel, but everyone was too excited to sleep.

By now the Civil War was struggling toward an end. The North was winning. On the day the Hodgsons sailed, Liverpool newspapers carried the news of Abraham Lincoln's assassination. Fifteen-year-old Frances watched from the deck as men loaded suitcases and trunks on the S.S. *Moravian*. The ship's bell clanged—time for visitors to go ashore. Frances shook hands last with one special friend. She had given her little dog, Flora, to this young man.

"Good-bye," he said. "I hope you will like America."

"Good-bye," she said. "You—I know you'll be good to Flora." He kissed her wet cheek and walked away, down to the wharf.

Then the ship began to move. Flora's new owner waved his handkerchief, and all the cousins and aunts waved theirs, too.

Frances felt hot tears spilling from her eyes. Softly she said to herself, "Oh, dear! Oh, dear! *Now* I'm going to America!"

✦ TWO ✦

Tennessee:
The Dryad Days
1865-1868

After three weeks at sea, the ship docked in Quebec, Canada. Frances first saw America from the window of a plush railroad car. To her, the new land looked green and beautiful. The trip from Quebec to Tennessee took two weeks.

Sometimes the train stopped for passengers to get out and stretch their legs. The Hodgsons enjoyed seeing new cities and meeting new people. They heard new kinds of English.

Knoxville was in the mountains of eastern Tennessee. Like much of the defeated South, it had been devastated by the war. Half-burned buildings still reeked of smoke, and farm land stood barren. Many men had lost arms or legs in the war. Amputation was the only way to cure an infected wound.

Food was scarce. Former soldiers and newly freed black people looked for jobs, but there was no work. Although the war was over, violence and death continued in Tennessee. Gangs of unemployed men stole what they could.

White property owners feared death at the hands of their former slaves. In reality, more black people were murdered, many by the newly formed Ku Klux Klan. This white terrorist organization began as a veterans' group in Tennessee in 1865.

Frances' uncle William still owned a grocery store in Knoxville, but business was bad. He hired Herbert, now 19, to work with him. Then he found John, age 17, a job in a grist mill—a business that grinds grain into flour or meal. The mill was near the small town of New Market, 25 miles (40 kilometers) from Knoxville.

Mrs. Hodgson and the girls moved to a log cabin in New Market. Frances felt like a character in a frontier novel by James Fenimore Cooper.

The Hodgsons' British way of talking sounded strange to people in Tennessee. With her sharp ear for speech, Frances soon mastered the local dialects. She began to use Southern phrases such as "I guess" and "I reckon."

Frances had expected to live graciously on a Southern plantation. But that life existed only in books. Here there were no servants. They had hardly enough money for basic needs. Herbert and John gave as much as they could spare, but the family was poorer than ever before.

To their New Market neighbors, the Hodgsons were a welcome change. Mrs. Hodgson had carefully packed the family's clothes and household goods and brought them across the ocean. Even though the Hodgsons were poor, they lived a bit differently from their neighbors. "...In a community where shoes and even undergarments were not always possible, [the girls] appeared with the neatest of sprigged muslin dresses, white stockings, ankle-strap shoes, and the tidiest of hair bound by gay-colored ribbons—and yet again, it was known that most of the time they did not have half enough to eat."

Their neighbors were glad to share. What could smell better than freshly baked biscuits, still hot from the oven, delivered by a new friend?

Fifteen-year-old Frances had blue eyes, a rosy complexion, and red curls. She was still plump, and quite short. When she talked, her lively expression was charming. She made friends easily. In New Market, she spent many happy hours with her next-door neighbor, 18-year-old Swan Burnett, son of the local doctor.

Swan was a shy, pale boy who loved to read. An accident with a knife had left him with a permanent limp. He amused himself by studying his father's medical books. Then Frances lent him novels by the British authors Charles Dickens and William Makepeace Thackeray. The two young people often read poetry to each other.

Swan wanted to be a doctor like his father. In 1866 he went to Cincinnati, Ohio, to begin his long study of medicine. He wrote Frances often during the years he was away. In her letters, she called him by the names of heroes in her stories. She never used the name Swan.

That same year, the Hodgsons moved from the log cabin in New Market to an even smaller house perched on the side of a mountain. Frances named it "Noah's Ark."

The closest neighbors were a black family who lived at the foot of the mountain. Frances asked Aunt Cynthy, one of their new neighbors, about the birds she saw. All Aunt

"It became one of her pleasures to lie or sit and watch a bird light upon a low branch quite near her..."

Cynthy could tell her was, "That's a bluebird," or "That's the redbird." But Frances longed to know their real names.

She wandered through the woods, and soon she could recognize the trees: sassafras, sumac, and dogwood, growing together over blackberry bushes. Frances often lay in the grass, reading, writing, or just daydreaming. Soon squirrels ignored her and rabbits hopped close by.

Frances was never happier than in these years she later called her "Dryad Days." A dryad, in Greek mythology, is a lovely, godlike maiden who takes care of forests and trees.

During the Dryad Days, Frances' stories took on a new tone of reality. The heroine's feelings became more important than long flowing hair and violet eyes.

Herbert and John were grown up now, but whenever they visited, they teased Frances about her writing. "Bosh!" they called it. Herbert always asked how she was getting on with her tale of "The Gory Milkman and the Blood-stained Pump."

Writing had become her lifelong habit. Wrapped in a

shawl, she worked in an unheated upstairs room. Her kitten Dora helped keep her warm. Often Edith and little Edwina came up to hear a new story. Pretty blonde Edith was Frances' most helpful critic. They were best friends as well as sisters.

Sometimes people gave them magazines. These were read over and over, especially *Godey's Lady's Book*. Its articles offered practical advice to the new woman, who had a mind and was encouraged to use it. Frances loved to read

GODEY'S

Lady's Book and Magazine.

VOLUME LXXVI.—NO. 456.

PHILADELPHIA, JUNE, 1868.

PHEMIE ROWLAND.

BY MARION HARLAND.

CHAPTER VII.

"FIRST a shadow—then a sorrow."

No one guessed how often Phemie said the words over to herself during the fall and winter that succeeded the brief brightness of her week in the country. Charlotte had been one of the berrying-party, and, becoming over-tired or overheated, she was seized during the night with a chill, that was the prelude to a hemorrhage more copious and protracted than and that had preceded it. So soon as she was able to bear the journey, they took her back to the city. She never left the house again alive. Throughout the autumn and the early winter, her longest journey was from her chamber to Phemie's on the same floor. Before Christmas she was bedridden, and required the constant attendance of Mrs. Rowland or Olive. One of these, or Miss Darcy, who devoted two nights each week to the pious charity, likewise watched from bedtime until daybreak, at the sufferer's bedside. Charlotte, usually yielding to a fault, was resolute in forbidding Phemie to undertake the whole vigil. The others could snatch an hour's sleep during the day. Phemie's time was not her own. It pleased Charlotte to have her best-beloved sister near her in the evening, although the busy, driven pen allowed the no opportunity for conversation. The golden hours of the twenty-four were those when the broad brow with the banded hair oversweeping it ; the great, thoughtful eyes and firmly-closed lips bent in the invalid's admiring sight over the paper she was preparing for Miss Darcy's magazine.

Phemie was a regular contributor to this now. The public were beginning to watch for her articles, and the principal editor to congratulate himself in place of regretting that he had obliged Miss Darcy by paying a new and

unknown author. According to his theory and practice she should have been contented, for a year or so, with seeing herself in print in his columns, and, in the event of her future celebrity, hold herself forever indebted to him for having furnished the stepping-stone to success. Phemie wrote nowhere except in Charlotte's chamber, and all she wrote she read aloud to this one partial critic.

"It is the next best thing to being an author myself," said the latter, one snowy December night, as Phemie folded and enveloped her sketch preparatory to delivering it at the magazine office in the morning.

She would save the postage by setting out early enough to call at Miss Darcy's on her way down town, and this was a consideration when prices were still on the rise and salaries in statu-quo.

"I wish I could tell you how proud I am of you, my precious sister!" was the addenda to the sick girl's comment upon the story to which she had been listening.

"I wish you had more cause to be proud of me, Lottie, dear!" responded Phemie, setting her desk aside and turning down the gas.

They could talk as well in a dimly-lighted room, and Charlotte liked to watch the play of the street light from below upon the wall. The speaker chafed her right wrist—what wearied penman does not recall the peculiar and sickening aching that led to the gesture?—and stretched out the fingers, cramped with their clench upon the barrel of a penholder for thirteen hours, with the intervals of two half hours for meals.

"You have not coughed so much to-night," she continued, perching herself upon the bed, and lifting her sister to a sitting posture by supporting her against her shoulder.

"Haven't I? I am glad! I dread coughing, because it must disturb you."

"Only as it gives you pain, my poor, unself-
499

Godey's featured articles, stories, poems, book reviews, sheet music, advice, dress patterns, house plans, and more!

the "Answers to Correspondents." Here the editor answered writers:

> Elaine the Fair.—Your story has merit, but it is not quite suited to our columns. *Never* write on both sides of your paper.
>
> Christabel.—We do not return rejected manuscripts unless stamps are enclosed for postage.
>
> Blair of Athol.—We accept your poem, "The Knight's Token." Shall be glad to hear from you again.

"I wonder how much they pay for the stories in magazines," said Frances to Edith. "I wonder…what sort of people write them?"

"Well," said Edith, boldly, "I've seen lots of them not half as nice as yours."

But Frances had no money for paper or stamps. How could she send a story to a magazine? "If we could make some money ourselves," she said sadly, one fine autumn day.

"But we can't," said Edith. "We've tried, you know."

"Yes," said Frances. "Embroidery—and people don't want it. Music lessons—people think I'm too young. Chickens—and they wouldn't hatch, and when they did they died of the gapes; besides the bother of having to sit on the hen to make her sit on the nest!"

"It would be awfully mournful," she continued, "if I really *could* write stories that people would like—and if I could sell them and get money enough to make us quite comfortable—and I never found it out all my life—just because I can't buy some paper and postage-stamps."

Edwina gave her big sisters an idea. "Aunt Cynthy's two girls made a dollar yesterday by selling wild grapes in the market," she said. "They got them in the woods over the hill."

Early next morning, the five girls set off together, each carrying a tin bucket. Picking and eating, laughing and shouting, swinging on vines—it took a whole day.

The Hodgsons earned enough to buy stamps and paper, with some money left over. But how could Frances mail a story? Herbert always took the mail back and forth to town.

"The Boys mustn't know one word," Frances said. "I'll tell them if it's accepted, but if it isn't, I'd rather be dead than that they should find out."

They turned to another neighbor for help. He bought their paper and stamps when he went to Knoxville. He let them use his name and address for the return address, to keep the secret from Herbert.

Frances wrote out a story that she had started in Manchester. She sent it to the editor of *Ballou's Magazine*, with this letter:

> Sir: I enclose stamps for the return of the accompanying MS [manuscript], "Miss Carruther's Engagement," if you do not find it suitable for publication in your magazine. My object is remuneration.
>
> Yours Respectfully,
> F. HODGSON

The story was not accepted, but Frances tried again. She mailed it to *Godey's Lady's Book*. Their neighbor brought the answer:

> SIR: [They thought she was a man!] Your story, "Miss Carruther's Engagement," is so distinctly English that our reader is not sure of its having been written by an American. We see that the name given

us for the address is not that of the writer. Will you kindly inform us if the story is original?

Frances wrote back, "The story is original. I am English myself, and have only been a short time in America."

The editor replied promptly: "Before we decide will you send us another story?"

Frances was overjoyed. Mrs. Hodgson's smile showed her delight. Edith and Edwina were wild. Dancing around, they shouted, "It will be Accepted! It will be Accepted! It will be Accepted!"

A happy Frances submitted another story as requested. The editor wrote back:

> SIR: We have decided to accept your two stories and enclose payment. Fifteen dollars for "Hearts and Diamonds," and twenty dollars for "Miss Carruther's Engagement." We shall be glad to hear from you again.

They were still celebrating when Herbert arrived. He had a new job working for a Knoxville jewelry store.

Frances asked Herbert to come out on the porch.

> "Well?" he asked.
>
> "I've just had a letter," said Frances, awkwardly. "It's—it's from an Editor."
>
> "An Editor!" he repeated. "What does that mean?"
>
> "I sent him one of my stories," she went on, feeling that she was getting red. "And he wouldn't believe I had written it, and he wrote and asked me to send another, I suppose to prove I could do it. And

I wrote another—and sent it. And he has accepted them both, and sent me thirty-five dollars."

"Thirty-five dollars!" he exclaimed, staring at her.

"Yes," she answered. "Here's the check."

And she held it out to him.

"Well, by Jove!" said Herbert. "...That's first-class!"

He never teased her about her writing again.

"Hearts and Diamonds" appeared in *Godey's Lady's Book* for June 1868. The second story appeared in October. At the age of 18, Frances was a published author!

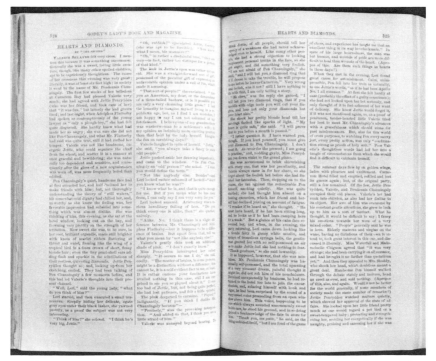

Frances' first published story. She used a pen name, "The Second."

Young Fannie Hodgson, top left, used her real name in Peterson's. *Editor Charles Peterson is at bottom left.*

✦ THREE ✦

Knoxville to Paris

1869-1875

At last! A way for Frances to earn money! Her stories began appearing regularly in ladies' fashion magazines. She received about $10 for each story. Soon Frances was writing five or six each month. From this time on, she supported her family by writing.

Most of her early stories were "popular romances." They were like the "Edith Somerville" stories she had told in school. Later she described their plots:

> Penitent lovers were always forgiven, rash ones were reconciled, wickedness was always punished, offended relatives always relented—particularly rich uncles and fathers—opportune fortunes were left invariably at opportune moments.

Stories like these, written in a standard way, are sometimes called "potboilers." They are written to keep the author's pot boiling, or to keep money coming in. Frances' potboilers were better than most.

In less than a year, she earned enough money to move her mother and sisters to Knoxville. They rented a rambling brick house on the Tennessee River. The house was run-down but comfortable. They named it "Vagabondia Castle."

Knoxville had changed for the better in the three years since the end of the Civil War. The town had resumed its prewar role of social and trading center, and had continued to grow. Before the war, in 1860, the population had been 3,000. By 1870, it had grown to 10,000, including the Hodgsons.

This period after the war was known as Reconstruction. All over town, hammers were banging, and the Hodgsons smelled new lumber and fresh paint. The burned-out buildings were replaced, one by one.

Frances called Knoxville "a curious little village [with] forests and hills shutting it in from the world."

Frances lived or visited in these places.

After three years in the country, the family delighted in parties, church socials, candy pulls, and boating from their own back yard. The three sisters were pretty and stylish in dresses they often took apart and remade to look different. Herbert, now a prosperous young businessman, brought his new wife, Ann, to visit.

The family loved music. Most any evening, their voices echoed over the tinkling piano, and the sounds carried far down the river. Frances and Herbert could both play. Edith sang well and so did Frances.

Other friends played a flute and a violin. Their cousin, Fred Boond, brought the bass viol. Edith's beau, Pleasant Fahnestock, played the clarinet, but not very well. The group called themselves "Bohemians," a slang term for people who were poor, artistic, and unconventional.

Frances was shocked when her brother John became a bartender. That was too unconventional! It was a disgraceful choice to the rest of his family. They lost contact with him.

The family lost another member in 1870 when Mrs. Hodgson died at the age of 55. Now Frances was the adult in the family. The 1870 census listed her occupation as music teacher, but she earned her living by writing. She was 21 years old. Her sisters were 19 and 17.

During these Knoxville years, Frances had a special admirer. Swan Burnett, her old friend from New Market, had grown into a tall man, with black-brown hair and "poetic" eyes. Most of his time was spent at medical school in Ohio and then in New York, but he visited Frances whenever he could. They wrote each other long letters.

Swan proposed marriage to Frances many times, but she turned him down. She would not marry him because she was not in love with him. Swan remained her dear friend, the only one who cared about art, or literature, or the world outside Tennessee.

After three years in Knoxville, Frances began to feel restless. Her sisters were happy, but she was not. It was hard for her to write new romances without repeating herself. She was exhausted from writing so many stories each month.

To Swan, Frances confided her discontent. "What is there," she wrote, to feed my poor, little, busy brain in this useless, weary, threadbare life? I can't eat my own heart forever. I can't write things that are worth reading if I never see things which are worth seeing, or speak to people who are worth hearing. I cannot weave silk if I see nothing but calico—calico—calico.

Frances began to save money for a trip to England. Swan did not approve. He feared that the men in England would find her beautiful and charming. She would probably be swept off her feet by a duke or an earl. But he could not stop her.

Frances' savings grew quickly, thanks to the generosity of a man she had never met. Charles Peterson, editor of *Peterson's Ladies' Magazine*, encouraged the new writer. He soon paid her more than he paid his other writers. Frances wrote later, "Other editors were kind enough to praise my work when they accepted it, but I did not find that their admiration caused them to add to the size of their checks of payment."

Peterson submitted her best stories to literary magazines. These paid even more. Frances was amazed that the famous publications accepted her work. Never before had she dared to send stories to *Harper's*, the *Atlantic*, or *Scribner's Monthly*.

In 1871 Swan Burnett finished his medical training and returned to Knoxville. He opened an office for his private practice, specializing in treatment of the eye and ear. He also worked part time as a hospital supervisor.

The handsome young doctor waxed his moustache and grew bolder. Again and again he asked Frances to marry him, but she refused. They remained close friends, and he became her business manager.

Left, Charles Peterson (1819-1887), editor of Peterson's Ladies'
Magazine. *Right, Richard Watson Gilder (1844-1909), Frances' editor
at Scribner's.*

Frances wrote a new kind of story in 1871. "Surly Tim's
Trouble" is set in an English mill. The characters speak in
the Lancashire dialect, which Frances remembered from her
childhood. The main character dies after an industrial accident. Frances said that she wept while writing it. She
submitted it to Dr. Josiah Holland, editor of *Scribner's
Monthly*, a literary magazine.

An acceptance came in February 1872. "My Dear Miss
Hodgson," wrote the assistant editor,

> Dr. Holland, Dr. Holland's daughter (Miss Annie) and
> Dr. Holland's right-hand man (myself) have all wept
> sore over "Surly Tim." Hope to weep again over mss
> [manuscripts] from you.
>
> Very sincerely and tearfully,
> Watson Gilder

Her next story, "Seth," about Lancashire coal miners, was also a tragedy. The miner hero dies of cholera, and only then do the other characters learn that he was really a young woman. Critics liked the surprise ending, and they admired Frances' ability to write in a regional dialect. The name "Fannie Hodgson" grew familiar to readers. Her stories earned more than ever before—enough to pay for her trip to England!

Swan was frantic. How could she leave him? Frances hated to see him suffer. He begged her to marry him—he would not take no for an answer!

At last Frances said yes. She would marry him—after she came back from England. Swan agreed to this. He had no choice. He wanted the marriage on any terms.

Frances took the train to New York. There she visited Scribner's offices, and met the assistant editor, Richard Watson Gilder. They liked each other at once, and worked together for many years. When Gilder learned that Frances felt embarrassed by her lack of formal education, he gave her a list of books to read.

Frances had planned to stay in England for just a few months. To Swan's dismay, her visit lasted a year. Would she ever come home? His love letters had no effect; Frances was having too much fun. She visited relatives and old friends, who celebrated her success. She went sightseeing and read the books on her list. All this time Frances kept writing and mailing her stories back to American magazines.

Sometimes she shopped for presents—dollhouse dishes and furniture for a little friend in Tennessee. For herself, Frances ordered a white satin wedding dress with a long train. It was to be shipped directly to Knoxville.

She returned to Tennessee in August 1873, to a joyous

reunion with Swan, Edith, and Edwina. Both sisters had married, and each had a new baby. Frances enjoyed being an aunt.

Her own wedding was planned for September 19, but when the time drew near, her dress still had not arrived! Frances wanted to postpone the ceremony, but Swan would not wait. This time she yielded. He had already waited seven years.

They were married in New Market, at the Burnett family home. Frances wore a corn-colored dress of flowered poplin. Swan's parents had invited a few close friends, and Frances' sisters brought their babies.

Later, Edith described the wedding. "The old-fashioned living room, lit with candles, had a sort of plain dignity, and after the simple ceremony, we went into the dining room for supper."

The newlyweds took a train to New York, for a honeymoon that was also a business trip. They met with R. W. Gilder, who introduced Frances to two famous writers. Bret Harte was known for his short stories, including "The Luck of Roaring Camp." George MacDonald, the Scottish poet and novelist, had just published his two most famous books, *At the Back of the North Wind* and *The Princess and the Goblin*.

Soon the Burnetts returned to Knoxville, to a small, rented house on a hill. Swan did not earn enough to support a family, and Frances kept writing. In the spring of 1874, Frances learned she was "with child." In those days, the word "pregnant" was considered shocking. Expectant mothers of Frances' social class were supposed to hide their growing bodies from public view.

Frances did not mind staying home. She hated the summer heat. When she felt well enough, she wrote, or

Above, portrait of young Frances. Now friends called her Fluffy. *After her marriage, she wrote under the name* Frances Hodgson Burnett. *Right, Swan Burnett from a miniature portrait, made when he was about 25. Frances married him in 1873.*

sewed baby clothes. She used fine cotton material called "lawn," and trimmed the tiny garments with lace.

Each stitch gave her pleasure, but sometimes she dreamed of the future. She was determined to travel and to learn more about the world. She began planning another trip to England, although she knew Swan would not approve.

Their son Lionel was born at home on September 20, 1874. The Burnetts hired an elderly woman, a former slave named Prissie, to help look after the baby.

The new mother kept writing to support her husband and son. It was impossible, she had learned, for an eye and ear specialist to earn a good living in a small town like Knoxville. Swan wanted to move his practice to a larger city, but he would need additional training. He wanted to study in Paris.

Paris! Frances longed to go, but how could they afford it? Then Charles Peterson, of *Peterson's Ladies' Magazine*, helped her again. When Frances wrote him about Paris, he agreed to advance her $100 a month. Frances would repay him with stories.

✦ FOUR ✦

Paris to Washington

1875-1884

The Burnetts, with Prissie and baby Lionel, arrived in Paris in the spring of 1875. For $34 a month, they rented a five-room, furnished apartment near the famous avenue known as the Champs Élysées. The Arc de Triomphe, the Cathedral of Notre Dame, the Louvre, Napoleon's tomb—all the sights they had read about—were just a short walk away.

But Frances was too busy for sightseeing. She had to write two stories a month for *Peterson's*, and she was writing a long story for *Scribner's*. "That Lass o' Lowrie's" is set in Lancashire. Joan Lowrie, the heroine, works as a pit girl in a coal mine. Tall and strong, she stands up to her abusive father. She cares for an abandoned baby. In the end, she marries a gentleman engineer. *Scribner's* printed the story in monthly installments and readers loved it.

Swan studied from day to night in Paris while Frances

wrote or sewed. She was expecting again; the baby was due in the spring of 1876. Frances hoped for a girl. She had chosen the name *Vivien* for a daughter.

Prissie took care of the household, and kept Lionel, now a toddler, out of trouble. Frances called her son "the roughest, biggest, tearingest rascal the family has ever known. He grubs and scrubs and a new dress lasts him just half a day." (In those days baby boys wore dresses.)

Lionel, she reported, beat his doll when it "refused to eat bread crusts," and used his toy lamb to mop the floor. When Frances gave birth to a second son, on April 5, 1876, Lionel suggested throwing him into the fire.

Vivien was considered a girl's name, but a popular novel of the time had a male character called Vivian. Frances changed the spelling of the name she had chosen and used it for her new son.

Soon after Vivian's birth, Frances resumed her heavy writing schedule. "I have worked like a slave when I ought to have been resting," she wrote to Edith. "There are four of us, so the miserable, obtrusive pot must boil." Swan regretted that his wife was the breadwinner, but he kept quiet about it. In the 1870s this was too shocking to mention.

When the time came for them to return to America, Swan and Frances had barely enough money to pay the fare. Frances took the babies to stay with Swan's parents in New Market, while Swan went to Washington, D.C. He would set up a practice in the nation's capital, and send for his family when he could.

Scribner's decided to publish *That Lass o' Lowrie's* as a book. It was the first of 60 books Frances would write. When she received the offer from Scribner's, she mailed the contract to Swan, who helped to negotiate a better deal for her.

Then she signed a contract with the publishing company. In this legal agreement, Scribner's promised to publish and sell Frances' book. They would pay her a small fee, or royalty, for each book sold. The book would be registered for a copyright under United States law. This meant that no one else could copy it, or publish it, or profit from it in any way in the United States.

Critics were unanimous in their praise. The book was a best-seller in America and England, but U.S. copyright laws did not apply to Britain then. Frances received no royalties from the British edition. However, American sales promised a steady income, and in Washington, Swan's practice was growing. Together their earnings could pay for a family reunion. Frances took the babies to Washington.

The year was 1877—a time of peace, hope, and fabulous

Vivian Burnett, Frances' younger son, age 2½. At this time the Burnetts lived in Washington, D.C., on I Street.

This 1880 photo shows Frances' Washington neighborhood. Her sons walked to local stores. Their favorite was an emporium with a table of penny toys.

new inventions. Like Knoxville, Washington was still recovering from the Civil War. The population was booming, and Congress had just spent $22 million to make the city look more like an important world capital. The broad streets were newly paved, but cows and chickens wandered freely. Poor people lived in shacks and shanties next to expensive new houses.

When Frances arrived in Washington, it seemed like a Southern city. People visited casually beneath shady trees. But social life grew more sophisticated as foreign countries built embassies and sent distinguished officials as representatives to the United States.

People were reading *Tom Sawyer*, the new best-seller by Samuel Clemens, who wrote under the name Mark Twain. Washington had its own literary circle, and from it Frances made new friends, like David Hutcheson of the Library of Congress.

In 1879 the Burnetts moved to a large brick house on I Street. It was three stories tall, with large maple trees in the front yard. Swan hung eye charts in his first-floor office. His test glasses filled several cases.

Frances chose a third-floor room for her study. Later Vivian described it as

> a magic place, filled with all sorts of cozy feelings and comforts for her boys and her visitors. It had a fireplace, with a black fur rug before it, and on that a big armchair that held a sleepy boy easily on a mother's lap, even when he had become quite big and heavy.

Scribner's gave Frances a raise for her next novel, *Haworth's*. The hero is a Lancashire industrialist, a self-made man who, like Frances, lacks formal education.

1215 I Street, N.W., Washington, D.C. Frances wrote Little Lord Fauntleroy *and* Sara Crewe *in her den on the top floor.*

Reviews were disappointing. Critics were tired of Frances' Lancashire stories. But the book sold well on both sides of the Atlantic. This time, to protect the copyright and royalties in England, Frances sought legal advice. In order to establish her right to be paid for the British sales of the book, she had to stand on the soil of a British dominion on the day of British publication. Since Canada was still under British rule, Swan and Frances made a quick trip to Canada to fulfill this requirement.

But British copyright laws did not apply to plays. There was no way to prevent British playwrights from stealing her material. Four different authors wrote stage versions of *That Lass o' Lowrie's*, yet Frances received not a penny from any of them. Newspapers began to comment on the problem, in England and the United States.

Frances wrote her own play of *That Lass o' Lowrie's*. It was produced in New York City. The play closed quickly, but Frances was not discouraged. She had enjoyed her first experience in the theater. She would try again!

Her next novel was an American story called *Louisiana*. It was very popular. She began to receive fan letters, and a wealthy reader in Cincinnati mailed her a silk shawl. Suddenly everyone in Washington wanted to meet the famous author. Her "Tuesday afternoon" social gatherings attracted politicians, judges, writers, theater people, and society ladies. Frances enjoyed entertaining and making her guests feel comfortable. Now she could afford to employ a cook and butler.

Frances still sewed for herself and her sons. She made the boys' party clothes in the fashionable style: velvet suits with lace collar and cuffs, pants just below knee length, and big sashes. For herself, she made elaborate gowns.

Her friends and family began to call her Fluffy instead

Frances (left) in one of her elaborate dresses. She told Vivian (above, in curls) and Lionel "hair-curling stories," to keep them still while she curled their hair.

of Fannie, perhaps because of her curly bangs or her frilly clothes. She was known by this nickname for the rest of her life. Sometimes she even signed her letters *Fluffina*!

A Boston literary club invited Frances to be the guest of honor at a meeting. Mary Mapes Dodge, editor of the children's magazine, *St. Nicholas*, and author of *Hans Brinker and the Silver Skates*, was also invited. She wrote Frances to suggest they stay at the same hotel. Frances also met Louisa May Alcott, the author of *Little Women*, on this trip.

Soon Frances was traveling frequently on business. People began to gossip about her long absences from home. Wherever she was, she wrote. "I am a kind of pen driving machine," she said. "Write—write—write. Be sick; be tired, be weak and out of ideas, if you choose; but write!" Writing and traveling kept her so busy that her sons complained they never saw their "Dearest."

By now, Swan's practice brought in a respectable income. He still managed his wife's business affairs.

Vivian was a handsome, intelligent boy who enjoyed his mother's guests. He liked to help at her parties. But Lionel was quiet and shy around grownups.

Both boys preferred playing outdoors, climbing rooftops or swinging from the branches of trees. Their best friends were two neighbor boys, Abe and Irving Garfield, sons of James Garfield, United States senator from Ohio.

Garfield ran for president when Lionel was six and Vivian was four. The Burnett boys campaigned actively for their neighbor. Hanging from upstairs windows, they yelled "Rah for Garfield!" to people passing on the street below. Frances was terrified each time she saw them do it.

Bicycles were a national craze in 1880. After Garfield won the election, Lionel and Vivian were privileged guests at the White House. Vivian told later how they rode their bicycles through the halls, "colliding with sluggish senators and cabinet officials who were not quick enough—or were too much surprised—to be able to dodge quickly the curly-headed gymnasts bearing down upon them."

In July 1881, President Garfield was shot in the back by a crazy man, who claimed he had been denied a government job. Doctors could not remove the bullets, and for two hot months, the new president lay dying. When he died, Washington entered a period of deep mourning.

Frances was sad for another reason, too. She and Swan were growing apart. Her new book, *Through One Administration*, seemed to reflect her own life. The story takes place in Washington. Bertha, the heroine, marries a man she does not love. He loves her, but she loves another: a soldier just back from the Indian Wars. Bertha stays with her husband for the sake of their children.

Frances took some chapters with her to Long Island, New York, in 1881. She worked that summer with writer Will Gillette, who would write many plays with her. *Esmeralda* was their first theatrical success. It played for 350 nights in New York.

Through One Administration sold well and pleased the literary critics. Frances grew more famous. But in the two

Gossip linked Frances with actor/playwright Will Gillette (1855-1937).

years to come, Frances often felt ill and depressed. She could hardly write. One doctor called her illness neuritis. Nervous prostration, said another. Ann Thwaite, who studied Frances in depth, offers a third theory in her book about Frances, *Waiting for the Party*: Getting sick was the only way Frances could rest from writing.

At this time Frances became interested in theosophy, which teaches that meditation leads to a better understanding of life. She also studied spiritualism, the belief that spirits of the dead can communicate with the living. She attended séances. Later she studied the religion of Christian Science. Christian Scientists believe in healing sickness by prayer. Frances also took a course of "mind-healing" in Boston. She stayed for long periods with some Boston friends, the Halls.

Frances was close to the entire Hall family. The mother was a former concert singer, now a teacher. All three daughters were talented. Grace (Gigi) painted, Marguerite (Daisy) sang at concerts, and Gertrude (Kitty) wrote poetry. Kitty also visited Frances in Washington.

People were talking about Frances in Washington and in Boston. She was often away from her husband and sons. It was unusual then for a woman to work with men. It was considered improper for a married woman to spend so much time with male co-workers and friends like R. W. Gilder and Will Gillette.

Swan disapproved of her activities, but Frances no longer heeded his opinion. She did what she wanted. There was no question of divorce; it was almost unknown in those days. Somehow Swan and Frances maintained a loving home for the boys.

In 1884, Frances' energy for writing returned. She started work on a new book.

✦ FIVE ✦

Little Lord Fauntleroy

1884-1886

*L*ittle Lord Fauntleroy changed Frances' life, for better, for worse, and forever. It was her first book for children, but it was popular with readers of all ages. This rags-to-riches story was published originally in parts in the children's magazine *St. Nicholas*. Readers could hardly wait to find out what would happen next to the seven-year-old hero. The book earned Frances more than $100,000. The play became a smash hit, earning her even more money than the book did.

Mary Mapes Dodge, editor of *St. Nicholas*, chose the well-known artist Reginald Birch to illustrate the story. Birch patterned his hero after a photograph of Vivian in his velvet suit. Velvet suits were not unusual in Frances' social set. But Birch's illustrations, and Frances' exciting story, created a worldwide fashion craze. Not everyone liked the style, especially not little boys.

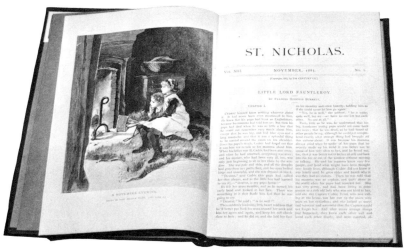

Scribner's St. Nicholas *was the most popular children's magazine in America and Great Britain. This is the beginning of the first installment of* Little Lord Fauntleroy.

The book was "marketed" like a modern movie or television series. Besides clothes, there were Fauntleroy souvenirs—playing cards, writing paper, toys, perfume, and even chocolate.

Fauntleroy began with a suggestion from Vivian. He missed his mother, even when she was at home in Washington. If Frances were writing, she shut herself in her study after breakfast, and worked straight through the day.

"Dearest," Vivian said, "you write so many books for grown-ups, that we don't have any time at all with you now. Why don't you write some books that little boys would like to read? Then your staying up-stairs wouldn't be so bad." Frances welcomed a chance to "make things even" for her young sons. In the evenings, she read them what she had written.

She based her new hero on Vivian. Her son was outgoing, with ideas that seemed wise for his age. "He was such a patriotic young American," Frances said of him. She had heard Vivian talking about presidential politics. "His remarks were so well worth hearing! I began...to imagine his making them with that frankly glowing face to conservative English people."

"When a person is a duke," Vivian asked his mother, "what makes him one? What has he done?"

Vivian did not understand the British system of inherited titles. In England, nobles inherit special privileges by birth. To Vivian, the word *noble* meant a superior person, someone both brilliant and kind.

Cedric, as Frances named her hero, is the son of an American mother and a British father. The father's father hates Americans, and disowns his son for marrying one. The young couple live modestly, with their baby Cedric, in New York.

Then Cedric's father dies. Some years later, when Cedric is seven, a British lawyer comes to his house. Cedric learns for the first time that his English grandfather is the wealthy Earl of Dorincourt. Since Cedric's father and two uncles are all dead, Cedric is the heir. The heir has his own title: Lord Fauntleroy.

Hearing the news makes Cedric turn pale. "Oh! Dearest!" he says to his mother, "I should rather not be an earl. None of the boys are earls. Can't I *not* be one?"

The lawyer has come to New York to find Cedric and bring him to England to live with his grandfather. Dearest agrees to this plan, even though it means she must live apart from her son, in a small house outside the Earl's estate. Cedric will be allowed to visit his mother, but she must stay outside the gates.

They travel to England. Little Lord Fauntleroy is amazed

Frances sent this photo (left) of nine-year-old Vivian to artist Reginald Birch. Right, Birch's Little Lord Fauntleroy.

by the riches in his new home, and he quickly comes to love the crabby old Earl. The Earl recognizes Cedric's unusual fairness and generosity from the start. The grandfather makes a special effort to please his grandson.

Cedric and Dearest meet their neighbors, and help the poorest people, as they did in New York. Cedric persuades the Earl to do more for his tenants, to build new cottages for them, to let a sick tenant stay until he is well enough to pay rent again. For the first time, people smile at the old man when he rides through town with his grandson.

Then their happiness is threatened. An American woman brings her son to see the Earl's lawyer. She claims to be the widow of the Earl's oldest son. She insists, therefore, that her son is the heir, the real Lord Fauntleroy.

When Frances read this part of the story to Lionel and Vivian, they grew very upset. "Oh, Dearest!" they gasped, "why did you do that? Oh, don't do it!"

"What will he do?" Vivian asked. "Won't he, Dearest, be the Earl's boy any more?"

"Shall I be your boy, even if I'm not going to be an earl?" asked Cedric.

Little Lord Fauntleroy continues as the Earl, greatly saddened, breaks the bad news to Cedric. Cedric asks, "Shall I be your boy, even if I'm not going to be an earl? Shall I be your boy, just as I was before?"

"My boy!" the Earl replies, in a shaky voice. "Yes, you'll be my boy as long as I live; and, by George, sometimes I feel as if you were the only boy I ever had."

Cedric says, "Well, then, I don't care about the earl at all. I don't care about whether I'm an earl or not. I thought— you see, I thought the one that was going to be the Earl would have to be your boy, too, and—and I couldn't be."

The American woman's son is proved an imposter, and the story ends happily when the Earl invites Dearest to come and live in the castle.

Like the Earl, readers admired Cedric for his generous, fair-minded ways. People were curious about how wealthy aristocrats lived. Frances provided luxurious details, and her readers imagined that what happened to Cedric could happen to any American boy.

Critics loved the book, too. In 1886 it was number one on the best-seller lists.

✦ SIX ✦

Sara Crewe

1886-1887

T he money from *Fauntleroy* paid for a larger house in Washington, in a nicer neighborhood on K Street. It had a skylight, a large square hall, and stained-glass windows.

One night Frances went up early to bed. She was reading quietly when she heard a great commotion in the hall. Swan rushed by, up the stairs to the attic. The house was on fire! A little boy passing by outside had knocked at the door to tell them.

Frances followed Swan with a pitcher of water. Neighbors and the fire department responded quickly. The Burnetts and their servants got out safely, but Frances was last. With flames roaring overhead, she grabbed her current manuscript and then she saved all the clothes in her closet. She loaded them onto the back of a man who came in to help.

The skylight collapsed with a crash. Firemen rushed Frances outside before she could save her shoes, or even find a pair to wear. It was a cold March night, and she wore only a nightgown and her Japanese kimono.

The house was saved, and family life soon returned to normal. Normal, for Frances, meant visiting her friends, the Halls, in Boston for months at a time.

At this time Boston was the literary capital of America. The Halls' parties attracted an international group of charming and well-read guests. Frances loved to meet people from other countries.

She still wanted to travel, and she especially wanted to take the boys to Europe. She longed to show them their British roots. Swan did not like the idea. He wanted his sons near him.

Meanwhile Frances finished another famous story, *Sara Crewe, or What Happened at Miss Minchin's*. Years later, Frances wrote a longer version of this same story, with a new title, *A Little Princess*. Both versions are still read.

Sara Crewe begins when the young heroine's father brings her to London. He enrolls her in Miss Minchin's Select Seminary for Young Ladies, a private boarding school. From the start, Sara dislikes Miss Minchin.

Sara and her father have come from India. Her mother is dead. Her father pays Miss Minchin a bonus to make sure his daughter will be treated well. Sara gets the best room. When the girls go walking two by two, Miss Minchin makes Sara walk at the head of the line, to show off her pretty clothes.

Then a terrible letter comes, saying Sara's father is dead. His fortune is lost. Sara is left with nothing.

Miss Minchin offers to let her stay and work. "Remember," she threatens, "if you don't please me, and I send you away, you have no home but the street."

Sara's fine clothes and toys are taken away. She is given an unheated attic room, and very little to eat. Miss Minchin makes her run errands in the cold and wet. The other girls laugh at her now that she is poor. But Sara's spirit is unbroken. She pretends that she is a princess. She thinks, "It would be easy to be a princess if I were dressed in cloth-of-gold; it is a great deal more of a triumph to be one all the time when no one knows."

She pretends her room is a room in a castle. Each evening she invents new details: a fire, a soft rug, books to read, roast chicken, and raspberry-jam tarts.

Sara "laid her doll, Emily, across her knees, and put her face down upon her, and her arms around her, and sat there, not saying one word, not making one sound." Illustration by Reginald Birch.

Sara makes up stories about her neighbors. She calls one man "the Indian Gentleman," because he is recently returned from India. Frail and ill, he lives with an Indian servant and a pet monkey. Sara, after years in India, remembers a little Hindustani, and speaks to the servant in that language.

Then one night, she finds a surprise in her attic room.

> In the grate, which had been rusty and cold when she left it, but which now was blackened and polished up quite respectably, there was a glowing, blazing fire. On the hob was a little brass kettle, hissing and boiling; spread upon the floor was a warm, thick rug; before the fire was a folding-chair, unfolded and with cushions on it; by the chair was a small folding-table, unfolded, covered with a white cloth, and upon it were spread small covered dishes, a cup and saucer, and a tea-pot; on the bed were new, warm coverings, a curious wadded silk robe, and some books. The little, cold, miserable room seemed changed into Fairyland.

The same thing happens the next night, and the next. Boxes of warm clothes arrive addressed "to the little girl in the attic." Miss Minchin lets Sara keep them. She is worried the girl may have powerful friends.

Then, one night, Sara finds a new kind of surprise in her room: the monkey! When Sara returns the animal, she tells the Indian Gentleman how she came to live in the attic at Miss Minchin's.

He asks her father's name. Then he tells her that he is her father's old friend. He has been looking for Sara to tell her that her father's fortune was not really lost.

Quite by chance, the Indian Gentleman rented rooms

Sara and the Indian Gentleman. Sara was like Frances as a child—brave and imaginative when life was hard.

near Miss Minchin's and his servant became interested in Sara. He got his master to pay for Sara's presents and he delivered them across the roof, through her skylight.

The Indian Gentleman recovers, and Sara goes to live with him. Their lawyer calls on Miss Minchin, who has submitted a bill for Sara's "expenses." The lawyer has a brief interview with Miss Minchin "and it is quite certain that Miss Minchin did not enjoy the conversation."

Once *Sara Crewe* was finished, Frances thought again of going to England. The boys were 11 and 12, old enough to enjoy a trip. This was the summer of Queen Victoria's Golden Jubilee Celebration—Frances wanted her sons to see it. For once there was enough money.

Heavy-hearted, Swan finally relented. They could go!

Frances with Luisa Chiellini, her secretary and companion. People looked serious in photos from this era. Cameras worked very slowly then, and smiles were hard to hold while waiting for the picture to be taken.

◆ SEVEN ◆

Frances Changes the Law
1887-1888

Almost directly, they were on the steamer in the midst of the wildest bustle and confusion; carriages were driving down and leaving passengers; passengers were getting into a state of excitement about baggage which had not arrived and threatened to be too late, big trunks and cases were being bumped down and dragged about; sailors were uncoiling ropes and hurrying to and fro; officers were giving orders; ladies and gentlemen and children and nurses were coming on board.

This quotation comes from *Little Lord Fauntleroy*. It could also describe the scene as Frances, Lionel, Vivian, and Kitty Hall, Frances' friend from Boston, boarded the S.S. *Ems*, bound for England. They were off on an adventure! Ocean travel had become faster, thanks to improved steamships. The crossing took about 10 days.

Frances attended Queen Victoria's Golden Jubilee in 1887. This picture shows Victoria's Diamond Jubilee in 1897, when Great Britain celebrated joyously again.

The ship docked in Southampton, on the south coast of England. Here people were celebrating Queen Victoria's Golden Jubilee. Victoria had been crowned queen at the age of 18 in 1837. She had now ruled for 50 years. Many ceremonial events were held that summer to celebrate the anniversary. Signs in shop windows saluted Victoria the Good, and her picture could be seen everywhere.

Frances, Kitty, Lionel, and Vivian arrived in London in May, and settled quickly into a rented apartment. The city streets were bright with flags, banners, and flowers. Souvenir shops sold special coins, medals, and plates, and even Golden Jubilee marmalade.

The years Victoria ruled, from 1837 to 1901, are known as the Victorian Age. Born in 1849, Frances is considered a Victorian writer. She loved her queen.

On June 21, 1887, Frances' party watched a special Jubilee procession. They had outdoor seats with an excellent view. First came horses carrying soldiers and more horses pulling carriages. Soon they saw the queen's special guard, mounted soldiers from India. Next came the queen herself, that stout, familiar figure. Victoria bowed graciously to her subjects. Frances was thrilled. The boys claimed not to be so excited as their mother.

In October they went to Paris, and Frances showed Vivian the house where he had been born. They went on to Florence, Italy, where Frances rented an apartment for the winter. She enrolled the boys in a French-Italian school and hired a tutor for herself.

Frances' tutor, Luisa (Lisa) Chiellini, became their new companion. She was a young woman, strikingly beautiful, with dark hair and eyes. She and Frances both liked fashionable clothes. Lisa taught Frances the French language and was her secretary for many years.

Scribner's published *Sara Crewe* as a book in 1888, and it was an immediate success. Frances became popular in Florence, where everyone also knew *Fauntleroy*.

Then she received alarming news. In London, an author named Seebohm had written a play version of *Fauntleroy*. It would open soon. Seebohm must have realized that public opinion would be against him, for he wrote to offer Frances half the profits.

She left at once for England, writing her own *Fauntleroy* play on the train. She had decided to take legal action against the thief.

Seebohm's play opened in London in February 1888. Reviews were favorable. Frances' version, *The Real Little Lord Fauntleroy*, opened in May. Frances' Fauntleroy was the famous child actress, Vera Beringer. In those days, girls often played the parts of boys. Vera had to sleep on lumpy curling rags, but she didn't mind.

Later Vera wrote:

> I remember so vividly the first performance of all, at Terry's Theatre, when Mrs Burnett sat in a stage box, and in her enthusiasm flung me her immense bouquet of pink roses. Such an exciting thing had of course never happened to me before, and I remember saying "thank you" in a burst of gratitude, whereupon she replied, "Bless the child, and she did not forget a single word!"

Frances' *Fauntleroy* got better reviews than Seebohm's. People flocked to see it, including Prince Edward, Queen Victoria's oldest son, and his wife Princess Alexandra. It was a great honor for actors to meet the royal family. Vera Beringer, dressed as a boy, could not decide whether to curtsy or bow. The royal pair solved the problem by kissing her.

Frances hired a lawyer to sue Seebohm in the British courts. He was accused of violating the Copyright Act of 1842. The law allowed a playwright to tell the story of anyone's book on stage, but said the playwright could not copy directly from the book.

Since many of the lines in Seebohm's play were taken exactly from the book, the judge ruled in Frances' favor. He ruled against further performances of the Seebohm play.

This law set a precedent for all similar cases. An author could now stop a playwright from making a play out of his or her book without permission. London newspapers praised Frances, and the news soon spread across the Atlantic.

The Society of British Authors gave a banquet for Frances. Other famous authors attended, and poet Alfred, Lord Tennyson, sent a telegram of congratulations. The Society gave Frances a diamond bracelet and a diamond ring to match, and a certificate of thanks.

In September of 1888, Kitty, Lisa, Frances, and the boys sailed for home. Their adventure had lasted more than a year.

Frances' bracelet was inscribed "To Frances Hodgson Burnett, with the gratitude of British Authors."

When their ship docked in New York, Frances was mobbed by reporters. They had heard a rumor that Seebohm had killed himself; did Frances have a comment? She did not, and the story was not true. However, it taught Frances a lesson: She was now an international celebrity. Whatever she did made news.

She sent the boys home to Swan in Washington. They were old enough to travel alone. Frances went to Boston to prepare the first American production of *Fauntleroy*. Elsie

Right, theater program from the Boston Little Lord Fauntleroy

Left, Elsie Leslie in Editha's Burglar

Leslie, a well-known child actress, played Cedric. Elsie had already starred in an earlier, successful play by Frances, *Editha's Burglar*.

Boston loved *Fauntleroy*. Oliver Wendell Holmes, Jr., who later became a United States Supreme Court Justice, took his daughter and two of her friends to a performance. "We had a most delightfully memorable evening," he wrote to Frances, "though we were all crying like babies half the time."

The New York opening in December was a smash hit. *Little Lord Fauntleroy* was the most popular play of the year on Broadway. Frances earned $700 to $800 a week from this play. *Fauntleroy* toured for years, across the United States and Great Britain. At one time, 40 theater companies were touring productions of *Little Lord Fauntleroy*.

Frances used the additional income to buy the family a new house in Washington, at 1770 Massachusetts Avenue. It had 22 rooms, which she furnished luxuriously. For her sons, who liked to experiment with machinery, she bought a small, used printing press. They promptly began a neighborhood business, printing fliers and advertisements.

When Frances was in Washington, she still held "Tuesday afternoons." But she traveled frequently for months at a time. Now newspapers covered her arrivals and departures.

Some reporters wrote about Frances' personal life. She was away from her family too much, they said. They poked fun at her elaborate clothes. They said she flirted with men. They called Cedric a sissy! They called Vivian a sissy!

Frances was furious. In a letter in the *New York Times* on February 10, 1889, she asked, "Is it or is it not of consequence that a statement published and copied all over the United States is untrue in every word and detail?"

Left, Frances' older son Lionel in his early teens. Right, Vivian, the younger, age 12. No more curls!

The *Times* replied:

> ...unless Mrs. Burnett can get the law to help her, the scribblers will continue to describe her personal appearance and dress in such language as it suits them to use, to tell falsehoods about her family, to hail her as the Empress of Bohemia, to say that she wears "vivid silk Kate Greenaway dresses" and is "encircled by an army of young men," although Mrs. Burnett may protest that she does not know what a "vivid silk Kate Greenaway dress" is and that the "army" which "encircles" her comprises only two "young men" aged respectively 12 and 14 years.

✦ EIGHT ✦

The Loss of a Son

1889-1890

In the spring of 1889, Frances sailed once again for Europe, with Vivian and Lisa Chiellini. Lionel, now 14, stayed in Washington. He wanted to spend the summer with his father and friends.

Frances, Vivian, and Lisa went first to Paris. Frances had promised to take Vivian to the World's Fair, the Paris Universal Exposition of 1889. Vivian had read about the fair in newspapers and magazines. He could hardly wait to see the dynamos, gasoline engines, X-ray tubes, cameras, plastics, telephones, and dazzling electric lights.

The single most exciting sight at the fair was its trademark, the newly completed Eiffel Tower. At 984 feet (300 meters), it was the tallest structure in the world.

From Paris, the three travelers journeyed to Manchester, where Frances visited her former teachers, the Miss Hadfields. Their school was closed, and now they barely made a living, renting out rooms in their shabby old house. Frances rented a larger house, furnished it handsomely, and turned it over to the two ladies to run. Frances often used her new wealth to help friends and relatives. She had never forgotten what it was like to be poor.

She sat one day in a beautiful theater, waiting for the performance to begin. The show was a pantomime, a program for young people. The air was full of excitement as ushers seated the happy children and their adult companions.

Frances let her thoughts go outside the theater, to the neighborhood around it. Children who lived there had no money for pantomimes. They had to confront real terrors: poverty, illness, cold, abuse. Some were beggars, running between carriages to ask rich theatergoers for a penny.

From that time on, Frances supported a group known as the Drury Lane Boys' Club. Its purpose was to provide boys with a place of their own, off the street.

She wrote to a friend: "…I keep saying to myself, 'Why did *you* deserve to be the one blessed by the Fairy Godmother? Why should you have everything, and they nothing?'"

Frances had rented a house in London so she could help with rehearsals of her new play. *Phyllis* opened at the Globe Theatre on July 1, 1889. Reviews were poor. Although the play closed quickly, Frances enjoyed a busy social season. Vivian escorted her to parties, where he charmed the British with his intelligence and good manners.

Frances found a new friend that summer, a handsome young man of 29 (she was 39). His name was Stephen Townesend.

Stephen was a medical doctor who wanted to be an actor. His family thought an actor's life was not respectable, so

*Stephen Townesend
became Frances'
business manager
in 1889.*

he had become a doctor instead. When Frances met him, he had worked for several years as a physician. He had traveled to China as a ship's surgeon. But he had always continued to act in amateur and professional productions.

Stephen still wanted to be an actor. He did not want to hurt his parents; his father was a minister in a church where some thought acting was sinful. But Stephen knew that medicine was not the right career for him. Now he had a critical decision to make: whether to take up acting professionally, or report as scheduled for a new job as ship's surgeon. South Africa was the destination.

Frances pitied anyone who could not follow his heart's desire. She was sure that Stephen had talent—she knew a lot about the theater. She blamed his family for wasting valuable years of his life.

The ship sailed for South Africa without Stephen. Frances, playing Fairy Godmother, hired him as her theatrical agent and business manager. He was intelligent, sophisticated, and charming — important qualities in the person who would represent her to the theatrical community.

Planning his career became her new hobby. She could hardly decide which of her friends Stephen should meet next. Or perhaps he could star in one of her plays? She was busy, healthy, and happy.

Lionel, back in Washington, wrote to Frances:

July 9, 1889

DEAR MAMMA:

I have not received a letter from you for about three weeks, but I suppose you have a great deal to do. Aunt Kate gave me the five dollars you told her to give me and I am ever so much obliged.

I had a very nice time of the Fourth. I had all the fire crackers I wanted and at night I had Roman Candles and Sky Rockets in abundance. Papa gave me one dollar and seventy five cents. DeVin [his friend] got off early from the office and we fired off firecrackers for the rest of the afternoon.

… Yesterday, Monday, July 8, 1889, was the day for the great prize fight between Sullivan and Kilrain for the championship of the world. Sullivan knocked Kilrain out in seventy two rounds. I suppose you do not care for prize fights, but you can tell Vivian about it.

Tell Vivian if he is not too much employed that I would like to hear from him, because I want to hear about the Paris Exposition and the other things he has been seeing. Tell him also that the Washingtons have won another game. They played it yesterday.

The score was 4 to 3, in favor of the Washingtons.

...Papa will leave Washington July 15 and he will leave New York July 18. With plenty of love to all.

Your loving son,
LIONEL BURNETT

Swan was going to a medical conference in Germany. He stopped in London for a short visit, then he took Vivian back to Washington. A new school year would soon begin.

Still in England, Frances moved Stephen and Lisa to a

"She talked a blue streak," said one observer. "But she was always entertaining."

house in the country. She had received the bungalow as a gift from the owners of a new housing development. To get publicity, they named it "Dorincourt" after the castle in *Fauntleroy*, and gave it to Frances.

Dorincourt was in the county of Surrey, south of London. The houses stood in a beautiful park, surrounded by woods, hills, and lakes. Yet London was less than two hours away by train. The housing development had a club for residents, with stables for their horses. Frances bought a chestnut cob to ride and drive.

She named the horse Gordon. The people at the stables thought he was dangerous, but Stephen rode him every morning with no trouble. Gordon also behaved well for Stephen when hitched to a high, two-wheeled trap, or carriage.

One day Frances drove the trap alone. She was on her way to the station, to fetch Stephen from the London train. At first Gordon behaved well. Then he bolted, throwing Frances out of the carriage onto her head.

When Stephen found no one waiting to meet him, he hired a man to drive him home. On the way they found Frances unconscious, lying by the road. Several people were trying to revive her.

Stephen had her taken to Dorincourt, where he took full charge of her care. His diagnosis: a concussion. Frances was unconscious for three days. It took months for her to recover, attended closely by Stephen and their friend, Dr. Owen Lankester. Nurses came from St. Bartholomew's Hospital to tend her.

Concerned about their mother, Lionel and Vivian wrote frequently. They had wired the house in Washington with burglar alarms, they reported, and with electrical starting devices for the gas lights.

The boys were still earning money with their old printing press. Frances cabled them $150 for a better, used press. Soon she began to receive issues of a weekly newspaper, written and published by her sons.

Then came bad news: Lionel was seriously ill. The whole family had caught "La Grippe," flu that swept through Washington that winter. Swan and Vivian soon recovered, but Lionel suffered a relapse. Then he had another, and another.

The news grew worse: Lionel was losing weight. His body was exhausted and sometimes his skin burned with fever. Then the worst news of all: He did not have flu—it was "galloping consumption." Now it is known as *tuberculosis*, and the disease is usually curable with good medical treatment. In 1890 it was the leading cause of death in the United States. There was no known cure.

Frances sailed for home in April. She refused to admit that her son could die. When she saw him, she made a special effort to smile and act cheerful, as if he would soon be well.

She took Lionel to a sanitarium, or health resort, in Atlantic City, then to another in Philadelphia. The treatment usually involved complete rest for the patient, and careful attention to diet and fresh air.

Lionel grew worse. Night sweats, a new symptom, soaked through the sheets to his mattress.

Frances gave up on American doctors and took her son to a sanitarium in Germany. Vivian and Lisa Chiellini went, too. Stephen Townesend and a trained nurse met their ship at Southampton and traveled with them to Germany. Stephen took good care of Lionel, as he had of Frances. But German clinics could not help Lionel, and he grew weaker. He coughed constantly, and his chest ached. His appearance was alarming.

A sad Vivian returned to Washington for the new school year. Frances, Lionel, Stephen, and Lisa moved to Paris.

Frances wrote often to Vivian. Their apartment was pleasant and homelike, she reported, but Lionel spent his days in bed. He could hardly eat.

There is no record of correspondence between Swan and Frances at this time, but Frances' letters to Vivian grew sadder and sadder. Lionel began to cough up blood. Frances, Lisa, Stephen, and the nurses worked hard to make him happy. They were good actors. The sick room was cheerful, even though their hearts were breaking. Frances wanted her son to have hope for as long as he lived.

Stephen, who loved Lionel, was the kindest of doctors. When he and Frances went to London on business, he wrote to the invalid:

> Boy, darling, good morning. . . . I am glad to hear good account of you from Nurse.
>
> You will remember the most important of the business matters on which your mother came to London. Well, the man she has to see is not in town, and will not be till early next week. But anyhow, it will only be some few days now until Mamma returns. We'll have real jinks then. Good bye, Dearie.
>
> Your
> STEPHEN

The patient spent his good days assembling model engines and pasting pictures in a scrapbook. On bad days he watched while Frances pasted. Soon there were only bad days.

Frances wore this mourning locket with Lionel's picture inside for years. The engraving says, "Farewell to others/but never we part/ Heir to my royalty/son of my heart!"

Lionel died quietly on December 7, 1890. Frances wrote to her cousin in Manchester: "Early in the morning he coughed a little and when the nurse bent over him she saw the end had come. When I spoke to him and kissed him he gave one little sigh and was gone."

He was buried in the Paris cemetery of St. Germain. The inscription on his tombstone reads "Lionel, whom the Gods loved."

After Lionel died, Frances kept this statue of him in her house. Now it stands near her grave in Roslyn, New York.

◆ NINE ◆

Life after Death

1891-1892

Lionel's death was reported in newspapers around the world. Frances was well liked in Australia, South Africa, Bermuda—anywhere English was spoken. Frances' books had also been translated into French, German, Italian, Swedish, and Polish. Now her friends and fans mourned with her; many sent letters of sympathy.

A grieving Kitty Hall took Frances to the south of France, and then to Italy. They stayed in the grand hotels. Frances decorated her rooms with pictures of Lionel.

Some people were surprised that Frances did not go home to Vivian at this time. She had been away more than a year when Lionel became ill. After he died, another year would pass before she saw Vivian.

But Frances loved in her own way. Her sadness at Lionel's death was overwhelming. She lost interest in living.

"There is only one place where I *want* to go," she wrote, "and I think I shall reach it—It is where Lionel lies among his flowers at St. Germain." Her only comfort was remembering that she had stayed brave and cheerful for him, right to the end.

Sometimes she felt as though he were still with her. She wrote to him in a notebook, as though talking to him in heaven. She thought of him constantly. With all her money, she had not been able to save him. But money could help other children; Frances always remembered the poor.

She worked now for the Invalid Children's Aid [Society], and for the St. Monica's Home for crippled children in London. Frances gave money and brought the sick children flowers and gifts. Then she learned that the Drury Lane Boys' Club needed a larger meeting room. She rented and furnished part of a building for the boys to use.

Frances gave the club a library, to encourage the boys to read. She bought copies of Lionel's favorite books for their library, and more. Frances knew the value of good books. All her life she educated herself by reading.

She forced herself to keep writing. "Giovanni and the Other," a short story, was set in Italy, where Frances went after Lionel's death. In the story, a wealthy tourist decides to support a poor peasant boy in memory of her own dead son. The peasant becomes a great singer.

Her story "The White People" tells of a young Scottish woman with second sight. This means she can see ghosts, or "white people." She falls in love with a young man who is dying. He and his mother are comforted by knowing the girl. Through her, they come to believe that the dead can remain close to the living.

Frances' book *In the Closed Room* was published with

"Come and play with me," said the coppery-haired girl. Illustration by Jessie Willcox Smith.

colored illustrations by the famous artist, Jessie Willcox Smith. In the book, a little girl named Judith moves with her parents into a large house. There Judith meets a girl with coppery hair. The girl invites her to play in a locked room. The children have a good time, though the coppery-haired girl is a ghost. She cannot lift things or be touched.

The ghost asks Judith to rearrange the furniture and toys in the locked room. The room used to be hers, she says. It has been closed, with covers on the furniture, since Andrea, the ghost child, died. Now Andrea uses Judith to send a message to her grieving mother. When the room is cozily arranged, with a doll in a chair and a book lying open on the sofa cushion, the ghost is satisfied. "That is how it looked," she says. "They came and hid and covered everything—as if I had gone—as if I was Nowhere. I want her to know I come here. I couldn't do it myself. You could do it for me."

Andrea's mother returns to visit the house where her daughter died. The two mothers go up to the locked room together, and find the door open. Andrea's mother realizes that her daughter has visited the room. "It is all as she left it..." cries the mother. "She has been here—to show me it is not so far!"

The two mothers find Judith, seemingly asleep on a sofa. But Judith is dead, gone to play with Andrea forever in a magic garden.

For Frances, getting on with her life after Lionel's death meant thinking again about Stephen Townesend's acting career. She wrote a play for him, *The Showman's Daughter*, and decided to produce it herself in London. Stephen, who had been so kind to Frances and Lionel, now seemed changed. Frances wrote to Vivian:

> ...Of course, Uncle Stephen takes care of my business and is very particular about things of that sort, but as for the rest, I feel as if I was the one who had to take care of him. He is so delicate and nervous and irritable, poor boy. But I have to remember when he seems to be unreasonable, that he was never anything but *perfect* to Lionel, and that he was his comfort and strength and beloved to the last minute...

Frances rewrote *The Showman's Daughter* several times so the part would be perfect for her "poor, overstrung boy." People began to gossip about the exotic Mrs. Burnett and her handsome leading man. But the play opened to favorable reviews. Stephen's performance was singled out for praise.

Vivian was a teenager in this oil portrait.

Their happiness was soon interrupted. The Duke of Clarence, Victoria's grandson and heir to the throne, died suddenly of influenza, at the age of 28. England plunged into national mourning, and the play closed. Stephen complained it had happened because he was "always unlucky."

Frances decided to go home to Vivian.

Frances was about 39 when this picture was taken. "She wasn't the silly, simpering sort of woman," said her nephew, B.C. Hodgson.

◆ TEN ◆

Rumors

1892-1898

Frances arrived in Washington on March 11, 1892. She was overjoyed to see Vivian, but we can only guess at her feelings for Swan.

Vivian, grown tall and handsome, was a junior in high school. He still earned money with his printing business, and now he published a small book written by his mother. This story of the Drury Lane Boys' Club was later reprinted in *Scribner's*.

Mother and son spent a happy summer together in a cottage by the sea at Swampscott, Massachusetts. Kitty Hall came, too. Vivian took pictures, went for walks on the beach, and learned to play the banjo. He wrote often to Swan in Washington.

Frances worked on her new book. *The One I Knew the Best of All* is the story of her own life up to the age of 18.

Today this book seems wordy and affected. Frances glorifies her own accomplishments. She refers to herself throughout the book as "The Small Person."

But the writing style did not seem so silly in 1892, and Frances' fans hungered for details about her private life. They liked reading about the Hodgsons' move to America, and the way Frances started writing. Reginald Birch provided illustrations, for which he was paid $1,000. These drawings are the only pictures of Frances' early life, or of Frances as a child. *The One I Knew* sold well.

In her second year of mourning for Lionel, Frances put away her black clothes and began to wear soft grays and lavenders. She still wore her mourning locket. She wrote her letters on black-edged stationery. Frances lived quietly now, refusing most requests for interviews. Newspapers had printed too many unkind stories.

But she could not keep reporters from writing about her. They criticized her trips, her friends, her marriage, her son, her books, and even her frilly clothes. They said she dyed her hair, and that she wore wigs, a fact her family later denied. Over the years, her name was linked romantically with the names of several male friends.

In 1893 Frances' sister Edith came to Washington from California for a visit. They had not seen each other for years. Edith had gone west during the gold rush with her husband, Pleasant Fahnestock. Pleasant, the young man who had played his clarinet so badly at the musical gatherings in Knoxville, had died of smallpox in California. Edith was left with two sons. She had married again, and had a daughter with her new husband. Now that daughter was dead at the age of six. The sisters comforted each other, and mourned their lost children.

Frances invited her sister to go to Europe, Edith's first trip back in the 28 years since they moved to the United States. Edith and Frances rented a large house at 63 Portland Place in London. It would be Frances' British home for the next five years.

The basement of the house had long, underground passages. These gave Frances an idea for her next book, *A Lady of Quality*. "What a place to hide the body of a man you had accidentally killed," said Frances. And she had her heroine do just that: Clorinda kills her former lover when she strikes him with her riding whip. He is trying to blackmail her. She hides his body in an underground passage and keeps his death a secret.

A Lady of Quality differed from Frances' other books because it was set in the 1700s. Some critics judged it scandalous. Clorinda gets away with murder, they said. She should be punished! Her bad language shocked them ("Damn *thee*!...I'll cut thy liver from thee! Damn thy soul to h-ll!"). They disapproved of her dressing and behaving like a boy in the first part of the book. Frances' writing also came under attack, especially her eighteenth-century language. But the book sold well.

In London, Frances' closest woman friend besides Edith was Ella Hepworth Dixon. She was editor of the *Englishwoman* magazine, and she had written a novel, *The Story of a Modern Woman*. This book was considered shocking by some for its feminist viewpoint. Frances, however, was glad to meet another woman and writer who dared to question rules governing "proper" female behavior.

Frances' best friend in the early 1890s was British writer Israel Zangwill. Gossips reported a romance between them. Dark and thin, with heavy eyebrows and wire-rimmed glasses, Zangwill was younger than Frances, and not so well known. They spent many hours together, sometimes late at night. They smoked cigarettes. In those days it was scandalous for a woman to smoke. When Frances smoked, she often held a cream peppermint in her other hand and took a bite after each puff.

Frances saw little of Stephen Townesend in her years at Portland Place. He was an actor now, touring with professional companies. But in April 1895, she needed his services as her business manager. Someone was putting on an illegal performance of *Fauntleroy* in Paris. Stephen traveled there to fight for her royalties, and, eventually, he won.

Then he returned to Frances, and straightened out her personal accounts. Running Portland Place took a lot of money, and somehow the wealthy author had overspent. Stephen paid her bills and put her on a budget. Frances was grateful for his help.

Soon Frances and Stephen began work on a new project, the play version of *A Lady of Quality*.

In 1895, while Frances was still in England, Swan Burnett left their Washington house on Massachusetts Avenue. He moved to a house of his own, several blocks away. The *New York World* reported that Swan had separated from his wife, and that he would sue for divorce. Swan replied in a letter that was printed in the *New York Times*:

DR. BURNETT'S STRONG DENIAL
No Truth in the Story that He is Seeking
for a Divorce.

...I can only say that it is a fake out of the whole cloth, and one that is an unwarrantable invasion of a man's family privacy. I don't know who originated the story, but I know that whoever did attempted to sell it to several reputable papers, who sent men here to the house to see me, and, finding what sort of fiction it was, refused to have anything to do with it. The man who wrote the story never saw me, and there is no more truth in this alleged interview with me than there is in the rest of it.

As to Mrs. Burnett's return to this country, I cannot say. Her work may keep her abroad all Winter, or she may come back before cold weather sets in. She has her work that she has to follow up abroad, just as I have to attend to mine here. That is all there is to the matter.

Vivian said dress was Frances' greatest "Indoor Sport."

Vivian as a student at Harvard. He became a writer like his mother.

Frances returned to the United States at the end of 1896, to spend Christmas in Washington. Vivian joined her. He was now a student at Harvard University. The *Fauntleroy* legend had followed him there. Vivian met the nuisance "head on… by seizing a light cane chair and smashing it over the shoulders of the first man who tried to bait him."

In Washington he divided his time between two houses, his mother's and his father's. Edith and her husband, Frank Jordan, had moved into Frances' house on Massachusetts Avenue. Sometimes Edith's sons, Ernest and Archie Fahnestock, lived there too.

After the holidays, Frances went to New York to

supervise a play. She sent for Stephen to help with *The First Gentleman of Europe*. He became the stage manager. *The First Gentleman* closed quickly, but Frances and Stephen were ready with another play—*A Lady of Quality*. Stephen played Clorinda's father.

The company opened in Detroit, with Stephen in charge. Frances chose to stay in Washington. On October 7, 1897, she received a telegram from Stephen: "Sorry to send bad news. Theatre burned to ground. Everything lost but I believe all our stuff insured."

Frances replied, "Splendid advertisement. If all insured means only delay not loss . . . Courage, comrades all."

The play moved to New York. Vivian joined Frances there for the opening. He looked especially handsome in evening dress. Frances wore an elegant black gown, trimmed with black feathers. She carried a black feather fan.

The audience liked the play, but Frances did not. She thought the actress who played Clorinda was wrong for the part. Reviewers praised the actress, Julia Arthur, and criticized the play. Stephen's performance received several favorable mentions.

The play closed quickly, and Stephen returned to England. Frances and Edith followed, taking special care to avoid reporters. A big story was about to break. Page one of the *New York Times* for March 20, 1898, reported:

MRS. BURNETT'S DIVORCE SUIT.
The Well-Known Novelist Had Her Papers Ready in Washington Before Going Abroad.

WASHINGTON, March 19.—Mrs. Frances Hodgson Burnett, the well-known novelist, to-day instituted a suit for divorce from her husband, Dr. Swan

M. Burnett....Mrs. Burnett is believed to have an independent fortune. Dr. and Mrs. Burnett have not lived together for two years or more...

It is thought Mrs. Burnett will remain in Europe until the decree is granted.

Frances wrote to Vivian at Harvard:

...many of my friends have expressed themselves strongly on this subject and finally I have decided that they are right...to be neither married nor unmarried is a difficult position...I have purposely avoided making my appeal upon any grounds which would involve scandal. I have put it merely upon the ground of 'Desertion', which Dr. Burnett himself made quite simple by leaving my house of his own will. I have always thought he did this with intention. This matter will be arranged privately and with dignity and it is better for both that it should be done.

Frances was too famous for privacy in this matter. Her close connection with Stephen was well known. The *New York Telegraph* said on May 25:

MRS BURNETT TO MARRY HER STAGE MANAGER. WEDDING OF AUTHORESS AND HER CO-WORKER IN A LADY OF QUALITY NEAR AT HAND. TOWNSEND [sic] A MINISTER'S SON. IS 35 AND HIS BRIDE IS 45 AND BOTH ARE WEDDED TO ART.

Frances, who was really 48, issued a strong denial. She would not marry Stephen!

ELEVEN

The Walled Garden

1898-1907

On a cold February day, Frances traveled from London south to the county of Kent. The train took less than two hours to reach a little village called Rolvenden. Why she went, we do not know, but the trip had an important result. Frances rented a country house. Maytham Hall became her new home.

It was just 10 miles (16 kilometers) from the sea. The roads were ideal for bicycling. Frances and Edith preferred a carriage for their afternoon drives. The cyclists were their friends, American author Henry James and British author Rudyard Kipling, who had rented houses nearby.

Maytham Hall was large, but rent was less than half that at Portland Place in London. The gardens (yards) were enclosed by brick walls built in 1721. After a fire in 1893, the Hall had been rebuilt in the "modern" style. There were separate buildings for the bakery, piggery, dairy, and stables, and a croquet lawn. A square tower on the roof gave a view of the English Channel.

At Maytham, Frances discovered a long-neglected garden, completely enclosed. Inside were fruit trees—apple, peach, pear, and plum. She could tell that the wildly grown trunks and branches had originally been trained flat against the walls.

Frances had the trees trimmed, and the weeds and thorns cleared from beneath them. Although she employed several gardeners, she dug and weeded, too, kneeling on a small rubber mat. She decided to make the walled garden a rose garden, with 300 rose bushes of the coral pink variety called Laurette Messimy. The project took more than a year to complete.

Then the garden became her outdoor study. She wrote there, wearing lacy white dresses and matching wide-brimmed hats. When the weather grew chilly, a rug or lap robe kept her warm. A flowered Japanese parasol provided shade on sunny days.

In her rose garden, Frances wrote several novels, best-sellers then, but now forgotten. In *The Shuttle*, a cruel, impoverished British nobleman marries an American heiress. He keeps her from seeing her family for years. When she objects, he says, "You will do as I order you and learn to behave yourself as a decent married woman should. You will learn to obey your husband and respect his wishes and control your devilish American temper." In the end her younger sister rescues her.

Another novel, *The Making of a Marchioness*, is about a Cinderella with big feet. Poor, but well-born, she is invited to a country estate to help with a house party. Three beautiful

Above, Maytham Hall in Kent, England, as it looked when Frances lived there. Right, a recent photo of the garden wall.

society women compete for the hand of the owner, but he proposes to the unselfish Emily.

The story continues in *The Methods of Lady Walderhurst*. Emily is pregnant, and a wicked relative tries to kill her so that he can inherit the estate.

In Connection with the De Willoughby Claim, set in the United States during the Civil War, tells of a clumsy bachelor storekeeper who adopts a baby. *The Dawn of a Tomorrow* is about a wealthy man suffering from an unnamed illness. He is saved from suicide by some London beggars.

Frances showed where she first saw the robin in the walled garden.

All these books sold well, but critics dismissed them as "formula fiction."

In her rose garden, Frances made an important new friend: a robin. English robins are different from North American ones, according to Frances, "much smaller and quite differently shaped."

She wrote, "He would take crumbs out of my hand, he would alight on my chair or my shoulder. The instant I opened the little door in the leaf-covered garden wall I would be greeted by the darling little rush of wings and he was beside me."

Frances loved country life. She won the hearts of her neighbors with her friendly, generous ways. They liked to see her riding through the village in a handsome carriage. Her two coachmen drew admiring attention in their tall top hats. Sometimes she gave rides and gifts to the children. She held parties for them, too, and she helped the poor.

As Frances' business manager, Stephen visited Maytham Hall frequently. He supervised production of the play *A Lady of Quality* in London. He negotiated a new, higher royalty rate with Scribner's.

But Frances and Stephen were not happy together. Stephen was moody and more demanding than ever before. He believed now that he had the right to control Frances' personal decisions. Vivian wrote later that Stephen took a position of "domineering ownership."

Frances was nervous and exhausted, whether she fought with Stephen or tried to do what he wanted. In November 1899, she sailed for the United States to see her son.

Vivian lived in Denver now. He had graduated from Harvard in 1898, and had secured a job as reporter for the *Denver Republican*. Frances wanted to visit him in Colorado, but she was not allowed to go. Her doctor feared the high altitude would be bad for her heart.

Luckily Vivian arranged to come to Washington for the Christmas holidays. He found his mother looking tired for her 50 years, and older. She had grown stout, but her posture was excellent, and she still wore elaborate dresses. Her hair was a new color of red, and she wore rouge like an actress. Makeup was considered shocking for "proper" ladies at this time.

In February 1900, Frances sailed again for Europe. Stephen Townesend met her ship in Genoa, Italy. There they were married. The news made front pages around the world. *The New York Journal and Advertiser* ran large headlines: "LOVE'S AFTERNOON IN THE LIFE OF LITTLE LORD FAUNTLEROY'S MAMMA. THE AMAZING MARRIAGE OF MRS HODGSON BURNETT, AMERICA'S GREAT WOMAN NOVELIST, TO HER PRIVATE SECRETARY, YOUNG ENOUGH TO BE HER SON."

Many people thought Stephen had married her for her money. To others—perhaps to Frances—the marriage brought respectability. Frances had tired of being the scandalous Mrs. Burnett. Ann Thwaite suggested in her 1974 book about Frances that Stephen blackmailed Frances into marrying him, by threatening to expose details of their personal lives.

For a while the newlyweds seemed contented. After a cold, damp honeymoon in Italy, they gladly returned to Maytham Hall. Both wrote novels. Stephen's, which sold well, was called *The Thoroughbred Mongrel*. It is written from his dog's point of view. Frances appears as a character in the book, Mrs. Flufton Bennett.

But the marriage could not last. Stephen, always gloomy

Frances pored over seed catalogs and wrote to other gardeners to find the plants she wanted for Maytham.

and irritable, became more unreasonable. Frances wrote to Edith:

> He talks about my "duties as a wife" as if I had married him of my own accord—as if I had not been forced and blackguarded and blackmailed into it. It is my duty to end my acquaintance with all such people as he suspects of not admiring him...It is my duty to make my property over to him...It is my duty to work very hard and above all to *love* him very much and insist on his writing plays with me.

Despite her difficult marriage, Frances kept writing. She rewrote *Sara Crewe* as a play, *A Little Princess*, during the summer of 1901. That same year, Queen Victoria died. Her son became King Edward VII.

Vivian came to England for a visit. He did not like Stephen, and he wrote to Frances, "Because [Stephen] is the head of your house, and because he has shown himself my enemy more than once, it would be both a task and a risk for me to sleep under the same roof with him and you."

Frances, Edith, and Vivian traveled through Europe together, then sailed for New York in December 1901. On April 10, 1902, the *New York Times* reported that Frances was "much run down," and that she had become a patient at a New York sanitarium.

Stephen followed her across the ocean. At the sanitarium Frances finally found the courage to tell him the marriage was over. His threats to destroy her reputation did not change her mind. She chose independence.

Stephen returned to England, to resume his career as an actor. He never fulfilled his threats to blackmail her.

Feeling better, Frances rented a house in New York City

for herself and Vivian. He worked now for a New York publisher, where he wrote "blurbs," or notes for the covers of new books.

Soon Frances was working too, rehearsing the play *A Little Princess*. It opened in New York in January 1903, to excellent reviews. In the summer of 1903, she rewrote it as a book, which was also well received.

Two more Burnett plays opened in New York within the year. *The Pretty Sister of José* was a hit, but *That Man and I* was a failure. Frances claimed she never read reviews of her own plays.

In 1904 she returned to Maytham Hall. She spent the summer writing in her rose garden. Friends visited. Some came in those noisy new contraptions, automobiles!

Swan Burnett died in 1904. He had married an old family friend four years after the divorce. Frances felt sad at his passing. She wrote to Vivian, "I keep thinking of him as he was when he was a boy, years younger than you...if souls do meet each other, who would meet him first but Lionel."

In 1905 Frances became a United States citizen. She had felt British from birth, and American because of her two sons. Perhaps the move added legal strength to her separation from Stephen. There is no known record of a divorce.

In 1907 her agreement to rent Maytham Hall expired. Frances decided to build herself a permanent home in New York. It would have to have a garden.

Two views of the house at Plandome. Frances wrote The Secret Garden *in her upstairs study. Roses and hollyhocks bloomed below.*

◆ TWELVE ◆

The Secret Garden

1908-1910

Frances decided to build her house on Long Island, New York, near the little town of Plandome. Long Island was farm land in those days. Cabbages, eggplants, and potatoes grew there. But it was just an hour by train from New York City. Vivian helped her find the right spot. They chose land on the north side of the island, overlooking Manhasset Bay. The view was beautiful, day or night.

Vivian, now balding and in his thirties, still lived in New York. He owned and published *The Children's Magazine*. Frances left him in charge of construction at Plandome, while she went to Germany and England. When she returned to New York in December 1908, the house was nearly done.

Just one novel, *The Shuttle*, paid for everything—the land and a sprawling white villa with a red tile roof, balconies, a large terrace, and stone steps leading down the hill to the beach. All this took more than a year to complete.

Frances filled her home with antiques, paintings, oriental rugs, and deeply-upholstered furniture. She had a dollhouse built in a large cupboard, to hold her collection. Her dolls had a grand piano, a carpet sweeper, a shower-bath, and a full set of servant dolls to care for everything.

Frances designed the garden (grounds) for her new house. Vivian reported:

> The spring of 1909 was full of the excitement and delight of making lawns, deciding on the direction of paths, the moving in and the planting of hundreds of trees and bulbs. By autumn, a real miracle had been accomplished. The brand-new house stood on its terraces amid green lawns, surrounded by shading trees and thickets of flowering bushes.

The new house was large enough for Frances' entire family. Edith and her husband, Frank Jordan, came to live there. Archie and Ernest Fahnestock, Edith's sons, were frequent visitors. Edith ran the household and took care of her older sister. She still liked to listen to Frances' stories.

At Plandome, Frances tried to write each day from 10:00 A.M. to 1:00 P.M. Her study was on the second floor of the south wing. Its windows were in the treetops. Through the leaves she could watch the sea or her flowers blooming in the garden below.

Frances' new book was about a garden. *The Secret Garden* begins:

> When Mary Lennox was sent to Misselthwaite Manor to live with her uncle everybody said she was the most disagreeable-looking child ever seen. It was true, too. She had a little thin face and a little thin body, thin light hair and a sour expression. Her hair

was yellow, and her face was yellow because she had
been born in India and had always been ill in one
way or another.

Mary is the unloved child of selfish, rich parents. Now
they are dead, and she has come from India to live with her
uncle in Yorkshire, in the north of England.

Mary's uncle is crippled and he keeps to himself. He is
often away for months at a time. He still grieves for his wife,
who died 10 years before.

Though Misselthwaite Manor has 100 rooms, most of
them are closed and locked. The housekeeper gives Mary
two rooms for herself, forbidding her to enter other parts of
the house.

Martha, a maid, makes friends with the unhappy girl.
She helps Mary to learn English ways. When she sends
Mary out to play, she tells her that one garden at Misselthwaite has been locked up for 10 years. Mr. Craven had the
garden closed after his wife died from a fall there.

Outside Mary meets a robin and a gruff old gardener,
Ben Weatherstaff. The robin helps her find the key, and then
the door, to the Secret Garden. Inside the garden, climbing
roses have grown over everything, and the trees and roses
look dead.

Mary shares the Secret Garden with her new friend,
Martha's brother Dickon. He shows her that the roses are still
alive. Together they prune dead wood and clear away weeds.

Late one night Mary hears a voice crying. She follows
the sound into a part of Misselthwaite Manor she has never
seen. There she finds a boy just her age, crying in his bed.
She learns that he is her uncle's son, her cousin Colin.

Colin is an invalid, confined to bed, unable to walk. He

fears that a lump is growing on his back. No one expects him to live to adulthood.

Colin was born on the day following his mother's accident in the garden, and she died after giving birth. His father cannot bear to look at him. The servants fear and dislike the boy, who acts like a tyrant.

Mary interrupts Colin one night when he is having a tantrum: "If you scream another scream," she says, "I'll scream too — and I can scream louder than you can and I'll frighten you, I'll frighten you!"

She demands to see the lump on his back. The nurse uncovers Colin's spine. "There's not a single lump there!" says Mary. "There's not a lump as big as a pin! If you ever say there is again, I shall laugh!"

Then, to cheer Colin, Mary tells him about the Secret Garden. She brings Dickon to visit Colin, and they secretly take Colin to the garden in his wheelchair.

In the spring the garden blooms, thanks to the children's work. Mary and Colin bloom, too, with pink cheeks, healthy appetites, and new feelings of happiness. Keeping their activities secret from the servants adds to the fun.

When Colin's father returns to Misselthwaite, he is surprised to learn that his son is outdoors. He walks outside to look for Colin. Near the Secret Garden, Mr. Craven hears children playing. Then a tall boy runs out through the garden door, almost into his arms.

It is his son, as he has never seen him before. At the end of the book, the reader knows that Mary, Colin, and Mr. Craven will form a new family.

✦ THIRTEEN ✦

The End of the Story

1910-1924

When *The Secret Garden* was finished, Frances and Edith sailed for England. Good reviews followed them. Critics liked the book, which sold well, but no more so than Frances' other novels. *Fauntleroy* was still the favorite by far.

In England, Frances rehearsed *The Dawn of a Tomorrow*. The play opened in Liverpool, where it was a great success. Then, again, a royal death closed all the theaters. The king of England died of a heart attack at the age of 69. King Edward VII, Victoria's son, had ruled for just nine years. His son, George V, became king.

Frances now felt healthy and well. With Edith she toured the German Alps, returning to Plandome in July 1910.

There Frances wrote *My Robin*, a short book about the robin in *The Secret Garden*. He was the same bird from her rose garden at Maytham Hall.

Vivian in the driveway at Plandome. He edited The Talking Machine Journal *for the new phonograph industry.*

Frances' next book was one of her most popular, a comedy, *T. Tembarom*. It is a grown-up *Fauntleroy* story—the hero, a poor newspaper reporter from New York, inherits an English estate and a large income. At first T. Tembarom's manners and slangy speech shock the British, but then his simple, democratic ways endear him to everyone. Frances based the character on her nephew, Archie Fahnestock.

Frances took the manuscript of *T. Tembarom* to Bermuda to work on it there. She went on vacation in the spring of 1911. This beautiful island, off the coast of North Carolina, was ruled by the British. A visit from Queen Victoria's daughter, the Princess Louise, helped to make Bermuda a popular winter resort.

Frances rented a white cottage called Clifton Heights. It overlooked Bailey's Bay, near the entrance to Castle Harbor.

Vivian wrote that the house was

> ...perched on the top of a quite steep slope, looking
> out over cedars and...commanding a lovely view of
> the water. Almost, as it seemed, under the door-step,
> in the close-to-shore channel, the big steamers came
> and went to America...

In the summer of 1911, Edith's husband, Frank Jordan, died in an automobile accident. Frances had loved him as a brother. Now she took Edith to Bermuda, where the new house and garden helped distract them. Frances wrote to Vivian:

> ...So Edith and I are going to have our favorite joy of
> "making" a house.—And it is such a pretty dear,
> with a lily field enclosed with oleanders on its left
> side, and a banana field on the right of its sloping hill
> side garden—and a heavenly view...And at the
> lower part of the sea garden—shielded by a white
> coral wall—are to grow the six hundred and seventy
> two roses blooming in one's face when New York is
> seventy degrees below zero, and London is black
> with fog or slopped with mud and rain. And on all
> this island there is not a motor or a train, or a smok-
> ing, rattling thing.

Frances was 62 years old. Sometimes she felt ill and exhausted. The world had changed greatly since her birth. Automobiles had replaced horse-drawn carriages. Telephones and airplanes made the world seem smaller. Even in their island hideaway, Frances and Edith could not escape the new, faster pace of life. Ragtime and jazz replaced the waltz. Skirts grew shorter, and a dance called the turkey trot scandalized the nation.

*"Some glimpses
of Mrs. Frances
Hodgson Burnett
as a motorist," from*
The Bookman
magazine, 1907

In May 1913 Frances sailed for Italy with her friends Gigi and Kitty Hall. They had decided to "motor" through the Alps, and Frances loved the new freedom of traveling by automobile. She did not realize this was her last trip to Europe.

The continent was on the brink of war. European countries were building their armies, and the countries were acting competitive and warlike.

But international problems did not yet affect tourists. Frances and her friends found it easy to ignore business and politics, even rumors of war. They concentrated instead on the lovely Austrian mountains they could see from their automobile windows.

At one stop Frances happened into a *Kino*, which means *cinema*. The men and women inside were drinking beer at little tables and watching an American movie. Although they obviously could not understand the movie's English subtitles, they burst into laughter and applause.

Frances was surprised. Like many people connected with the theater, she did not care for moving pictures. Until now she had always refused requests to make movies of her works. The play *Little Lord Fauntleroy* was still touring widely, and her agent advised that moving pictures took customers away from plays.

Now Frances realized that movies had universal appeal. The film industry needed good stories, and Frances was always willing to earn more money. She sold the film rights to *The Dawn of a Tomorrow*. Success was guaranteed when Mary Pickford was cast as the heroine. Mary Pickford was "America's Sweetheart," the most famous female star of silent pictures. Long golden curls were her trademark. She specialized in parts for young girls, even after she was grown up.

Mary Pickford also starred in the second Burnett film, *Esmeralda*. Both movies did well. Frances sold film rights to four more books: *Little Lord Fauntleroy*, *A Lady of Quality*, *A Little Princess*, and *The Pretty Sister of José*.

Vivian met Frances at the dock when she returned to America in May 1914. "LORD FAUNTLEROY GREETS MOTHER," said the *New York Telegraph*. That same month,

Stephen Townesend died of pneumonia. He was only 54.

In June war broke out in Europe. Soon Germany and Austria-Hungary were fighting against France, Great Britain, and Russia. The Great War, today called World War I, had begun.

There was good news, too, that summer: Vivian was engaged! Constance Buel was 21, beautiful, talented, and musical. Her father was an old friend, Clarence Clough Buel, associate editor of *Century* magazine. Constance and Vivian married in November and took their honeymoon on one of the first ships to pass through the new Panama Canal. Frances paid for their four-month tour of Hawaii, Japan, and China.

In 1915 Frances published a new book for children, *The Lost Prince*. When Frances read it aloud to her sister, Edith said it made the blood race through her veins. In the book, two beggar boys travel to various European capitals. One is a street urchin, the other, the son of a prince. Together the boys help restore the prince to his rightful position as ruler of the imaginary nation of Samavia.

In 1916 Frances' personal life made headlines again. Edith's son, Archie Fahnestock, had married a woman named Annie Prall. Frances built them a house near hers. She thought Edith would always be welcome there. But the three of them did not get along. Annie accused Edith of making trouble, and Edith left. Frances was furious!

She wrote to Annie's sister, calling Annie "a liar, a slanderer, an ill-bred meddler, . . . a shrew and a brawler," and other names. Annie and her sister sued Frances, claiming the untruths she wrote caused scandal and disgrace. They asked for $50,000. The letter was made public when they filed the suit.

"MRS. BURNETT'S PEN TURNED UPON NIECE,"

said the headlines in the *New York Times*. Part of the letter was reprinted there. In court, Frances' lawyers said that Annie and her sister caused the scandal themselves by making a private letter public. The defense suggested that perhaps they wanted more money from a rich woman who had been generous to both.

The case lasted for two years, with two trials. In the end, Frances won, but public opinion was against her. Reporters made fun of her plump figure, ornate clothes, and artificially red curls. They called her books potboilers and the author a "high priestess...of the second rate." They said she was pompous and vain. Frances was hurt by their claims. She renewed her efforts to live quietly and avoid reporters.

During the war, Frances entertained servicemen and wrote them letters. She collected books for a library for British service men and their dependents stationed in Bermuda.

She received this letter from a British soldier:

> Am just writing this in a spare minute to thank you for writing *T. Tembarom*. It was lent to me when I had gone sick, and was, in addition, most completely fed up with life in general.
>
> It was a splendid tonic, your novel—it is a real bucker, and braced me up tophole. I should like to receive three such books every week. I hope it has done dozens of gloomy beggars as much good as it did me.
>
> [Signed] One of the
> Mesopot. Expeditionary Force, Baghdad

In 1916 Frances' granddaughter Verity was born. Dorinda, her second grandchild, came two years later. Frances adored the little girls, and they loved to visit their "Nanda" in the house at Plandome.

"Nanda" (Frances) and Verity at Plandome. Frances liked to play dolls with her granddaughters.

Frances' next book was a two-volume set, published in 1922. *The Head of the House of Coombe* told of a frivolous young widow named Feather, left penniless in England on the eve of The Great War. In the second volume, *Robin*, Feather dies when she rushes outside to watch the German zeppelins bombing London. All that is left is her hand, with a ring and a purple scarf. Frances' fans loved the books, but critics did not.

In the years following the war, Frances was almost always ill. Her heart was weak. She suffered great pain from intestinal attacks, and sometimes found it so hard to breathe she had to be given extra oxygen. In 1921 she appeared publicly for the last time, in New York City. She attended the opening of Mary Pickford's movie, *Little Lord Fauntleroy*.

In the movie version of *Fauntleroy*, Mary Pickford played a boy for the first time. Her curls seemed perfect for Cedric. With her hair pinned up, she also played Cedric's mother.

Some thought Mary Pickford was too old (27) and too plump to play Fauntleroy in the 1921 movie.

This double role was a new achievement in movie special effects. Mother and son appeared together in many scenes. Dearest looked nine inches taller than Cedric because she walked on ramps or wore nine-inch platform shoes under her long dresses. A closeup showed Cedric jumping into his mother's arms, and kissing her on the cheek. The 3-second kiss took 15 hours to film.

In her last illness, Frances worked on *In the Garden*, a book that was published after her death. She wrote on blue-lined tablets, sitting up in her bed. Her family delivered sharpened pencils to her second-story room. She was very weak.

From her windows she could see the leaves changing color, and her beloved garden below. The grounds were bright with roses, marigolds, chrysanthemums, snapdragons, and dahlias that looked like stars. Beyond them was the blue bay. The air smelled of flowers, and of the sea.

Frances died quietly at home on October 29, 1924.

❖ FOURTEEN ❖

Epilogue

Frances' obituary appeared in the *New York Times*:

FRANCES HODGSON BURNETT, AUTHOR,
DIES AT 74
ROMANCE IN EARLY LIFE
As a Child She Sold Berries to Buy
Paper and Pencil—Won First Fame
With "That Lass of Lowrie's."

The article praised *Little Lord Fauntleroy*, but did not mention *The Secret Garden*.

Frances was buried in the cemetery at Roslyn, Long Island. Near her grave stands a life-sized statue of Lionel. Vivian had it moved to the cemetery after her death. Sometimes, by mistake, people call the statue Little Lord Fauntleroy.

In New York City, a statue was erected in Central Park in memory of Frances. Sculptor Bessie Potter Vonnoh portrayed a boy and a girl in bronze. Across from the statue is a story-teller's bench.

Vivian wrote a biography of his mother several years after her death. *The Romantick Lady* shows that Vivian admired Frances greatly. But the book is also surprisingly frank about her life. *The Romantick Lady* was one of the main sources for this book you are reading.

Fauntleroy's fame continued long after Frances' death. The book has never been out of print. The artist Reginald Birch complained some years later, "They will still insist about talking about Fauntleroy. All my work of better quality has been pushed into the background."

When Vivian was in his sixties, and quite bald, he

Vivian, left, died a hero in 1937. Reginald Birch, right, illustrated many of Frances' works.

attended a luncheon with Mary Pickford. Both of them were well known as Fauntleroy. The master of ceremonies asked "the original Little Lord Fauntleroy" to make a speech.

"Mary," said Vivian, touching his head with his hand, "*this* time the curls are on *you!*"

A new film version of *Little Lord Fauntleroy* was made in 1936, starring famous child actor Freddie Bartholomew.

Vivian died a hero in 1937. He collapsed after helping to save four lives. "ORIGINAL 'FAUNTLEROY' DIES IN BOAT AFTER HELPING RESCUE 4 IN SOUND," said the headlines. "Vivian Burnett, Author's Son who Devoted Life to Escaping 'Sissified' Role, is Stricken at Helm — Manoeuvres Yawl to get 2 Men and 2 Women from Overturned Craft, Then Collapses."

In the years following Vivian's death, Hollywood filmed new versions of other Burnett books. In 1939 Shirley Temple starred in *The Little Princess*. Margaret O'Brien played Mary Lennox in *The Secret Garden* (1949).

The hundredth anniversary of Frances' birth fell in 1949. *Life Magazine* published an article, not about Frances, but about *Fauntleroy*. The article contained a picture of Vivian in his velvet suit, and photos of actors who had played Cedric. *Fauntleroy* was still Frances' most famous book.

Then critics began to notice *The Secret Garden*. In 1950 it was still in print, and widely available in libraries and bookstores. Artist Tasha Tudor provided illustrations for a new edition in 1962. Soon *The Secret Garden* was called a classic, then a masterpiece. Literature classes began to study it. Many children named it as their favorite book.

New technology brought Frances additional fame. Her movies are shown often on television, and recently became available on videocassette. New color versions of the stories

Little Lord Fauntleroy *as played by Freddie Bartholomew (above) and Ricky Schroder (right). Margaret O'Brien (below) starred in the 1949 film* The Secret Garden.

were produced in the 1980s: *Little Lord Fauntleroy* as a made-for-TV movie starring Ricky Schroder and Alec Guiness, and British productions of *A Little Princess* and *The Secret Garden*.

The Secret Garden is still one of the best-known, best-selling books for children in the English language. Four publishers issued new editions of *The Secret Garden* in 1989 alone.

Once Frances was a famous celebrity, the best-selling author in the world. Now readers know her through just a few of her books. Frances wrote, near the end of her life:

When you have a Garden
You Have a Future
And when you have a Future
You are Alive!

Her most famous garden, *The Secret Garden*, guarantees her a future that she could not have predicted, well into the 21st century.

Major Sources for This Book

Bixler, Phyllis. *Frances Hodgson Burnett*. Boston: Twayne, 1984. (Twayne's English Authors Series.)

Burnett, Constance Buel. *Happily Ever After: A Portrait of Frances Hodgson Burnett*. New York: Vanguard, 1965.

Burnett, Frances Hodgson. Letters. Scribner Collection, Princeton University Library.

Burnett, Frances Hodgson. *The One I Knew the Best of All: A Memory of the Mind of a Child*. New York: Scribner, 1893. Ayer, 1980.

Burnett, Vivian. *The Romantick Lady: The Life Story of an Imagination*. New York: Scribner, 1927.

Deupree, Penny (great-granddaughter of Frances Hodgson Burnett). Interviews with Jean Shirley. October, 1989.

Thwaite, Ann. *Waiting for the Party: The Life of Frances Hodgson Burnett 1849-1924*. New York: Scribner, 1974. Godine, 1990.

Other sources are Frances Hodgson Burnett's novels and stories for adults and children, as cited in the text or in the further reading lists below. A few of her books are still in print, but many others should be available in any large library. A list of sources for quotes is on pages 127 and 128.

For Further Reading

Frances Hodgson Burnett's Books for Children
A Selected List

Editha's Burglar: A Story for Children. Boston: Jordan Marsh, 1888. Seven-year-old Editha surprises a burglar. She helps him so that he will not wake her mother. Later he returns her things.

Giovanni and the Other; Children Who Have Made Stories. New York: Scribner, 1892. British edition, *Children I Have Known*. London: J.R. Osgood; London: McIlvaine, 1892.

In the Closed Room. New York: McClure, Phillips & Co., 1904.

Little Lord Fauntleroy. New York: Scribner; London: Warne, 1886. Many editions now available.

A Little Princess: Being the Whole Story of Sara Crewe Now Told for the First Time. New York: Scribner; London: Warne, 1905. Many editions now available.

The Lost Prince. New York: Century; London: Hodder & Stoughton, 1915. Penguin, 1986.

My Robin. New York: Stokes, 1912; London: Putnam, 1913.

Piccino and Other Child Stories. New York: Scribner, 1894. British edition, *The Captain's Youngest.* London: Warne, 1894. Short stories set mostly in Italy.

Racketty-Packetty House; as told by Queen Crosspatch. New York: Century, 1906; London: Warne, 1907. (Queen Crosspatch series) The poor but fun-loving dolls of Racketty-Packetty House were based on a family Frances knew. They meet snobbish new dolls from Tidy Castle.

Sara Crewe, or What Happened at Miss Minchin's. New York: Scribner, 1888; London: Fisher Unwin, 1887. Many editions now available.

The Secret Garden. New York: Stokes; London: Heinemann, 1911. Many editions now available.

Frances Hodgson Burnett's Books for Adults
A Selected List

The Dawn of a Tomorrow. New York: Scribner, 1906.

Haworth's. New York: Scribner, 1879.

The Head of the House of Coombe. New York: Stokes, 1922.

In Connection with the De Willoughby Claim. New York: Scribner, 1899.

In the Garden. New York: Medici Society, 1925.

A Lady of Quality. New York: Scribner, 1896.

Louisiana. New York: Scribner, 1880.

The Making of a Marchioness. New York: Stokes, 1901.

The Methods of Lady Walderhurst. New York: Stokes, 1901.

The Pretty Sister of José. New York: Scribner, 1889.

Robin. New York: Stokes, 1922.

The Shuttle. New York: Stokes, 1907.

Surly Tim and Other Stories. New York: Scribner, 1877.

T. Tembarom. New York: Stokes, 1913.

That Lass o' Lowrie's. New York: Scribner, 1877.

Through One Administration. Boston: Osgood, 1883.

The White People. New York: Harper, 1917.

Index

Alcott, Louisa May, 46
Arthur, Julia, 91
Atlantic magazine, 33
Aunt Cynthy, 21-22, 24-25
Authors, Society of. *See* Society of British Authors

Ballou's Magazine, 25
Bartholomew, Freddie, 119
Beringer, Vera, 64
Bermuda, 108-109, 113
Birch, Reginald, 49, 86, 118
Boond, Fred, 32
Boond, William, 20
Boston, Massachusetts, 45, 48, 56, 66-67
Buel, Clarence Clough, 112
Burnett, Constance Buel, 112
Burnett, Dorinda, 113
Burnett, Frances Hodgson: accident with horse, 74; appearance, 10, 21, 44-45, 86, 91, 98, 113; birth, 11; death, 116; divorce, 48, 88, 91-92, 101; "Dryad Days," 21-22; first published, 25-27; illness, 48, 97, 98, 100, 109, 115, 116; letters, 25, 26, 32-33, 40, 67, 70, 77, 82, 91, 92, 100, 101, 109, 112; mourning for Lionel, 77, 79-80, 82, 86; religious beliefs, 48, 80-82; schooling, 12, 13, 35; separation from Swan, 88; trips to Europe, 33, 35, 38, 39-40, 56, 59-65, 69-75, 75-83, 87-90, 91-97, 98-100, 101, 103, 107, 110-111; U.S. citizen, 101; wedding, 36, 98
Burnett, Lionel, 40, 44, 46, 53, 59-65, 66, 67, 69, 74, 101, 117; birth, 38; correspondence with Frances, 72-73, 74; death and its effect on Frances, 77, 79-80, 82, 86;

illness, 75-76
Burnett, Swan, 32-36, 38-41, 43, 44, 46, 48, 55-56, 59, 66, 69, 72, 73, 75, 85; correspondence with Frances, 21, 32-33, 35, 76; death, 101; divorce, 91-92; meets Frances, 21; separation from Frances, 88-89; weds Frances, 36
Burnett, Verity, 113
Burnett, Vivian, 43, 44, 46, 53, 59-65, 66, 67, 69-73, 74, 75, 79, 83, 85, 90, 91, 97-98, 100-101, 103, 109, 111; biography of Frances, 118; birth, 40; correspondence, 74, 76, 82, 85, 92, 100, 101, 109; death, 119; at Harvard, 90, 92, 97; and *Fauntleroy*, 49, 50-51, 53, 90, 111, 118-119; wedding, 112

Canada, 19, 44
Chiellini, Luisa (Lisa), 63, 69-75, 75-77
The Children's Magazine, 103
Civil War, 15, 16, 18, 19-20, 30, 42
Clemens, Samuel, 42
Cooper, James Fenimore, 13, 20
copyright, 41, 44; applied to plays, 44, 63-65
critics' reaction to Frances' work, 35, 41, 44, 47, 54, 64, 70, 82, 87, 91, 97, 101, 107, 115

The Dawn of a Tomorrow, 96, 107, 111
Denver Republican, 97
Dickens, Charles, 13, 21
Dodge, Mary Mapes, 45-46, 49
"Dorincourt," Surrey, England, 74
Drury Lane Boys' Club, 70, 80, 85

"Edith Somerville," 13, 29

Editha's Burglar, 67
England, 9-18, 33, 35, 41, 44, 59,
    61-65, 69-75, 76, 82, 83, 88, 91,
    93-97, 98-100, 101, 103, 107, 112.
    See also place names
Esmeralda, 47, 111

Fahnestock, Annie Prall, 112-113
Fahnestock, Archie, 90, 104,
    108, 112
Fahnestock, Edith. *See* Hodgson,
    Edith
Fahnestock, Ernest, 90, 104
Fahnestock, Pleasant, 32, 86
films of Frances' works, 111, 115-116,
    119-121
The First Gentleman of Europe, 91
France, 38-40, 63, 69, 76-77, 79, 112

gardens and gardening, 9-10, 94, 97,
    101, 103-104, 109, 116, 121
Garfield family, 46-47
Germany, 75-76, 103, 107, 112
Gilder, Richard Watson, 34, 35,
    36, 48
Gillette, Will, 47, 48
"Giovanni and the Other," 80
Godey's Lady's Book, 23-24, 25-27
gossip about Frances, 46, 48, 66,
    67-68, 82, 86, 87-89, 92, 98
Great War. *See* World War I
Guiness, Alec, 121

Hadfields, 13, 69-70
Hall family, 48, 56
Hall, Gertrude (Kitty), 48, 61-65,
    79, 85, 110
Hall, Grace (Gigi), 48, 110
Hans Brinker and the Silver Skates,
    45
Harper's, 33
Harte, Bret, 36
Haworth's, 43
The Head of the House of Coombe, 114

"Hearts and Diamonds," 26-27
Hepworth Dixon, Ella, 87
Hodgson, Edith, 12, 13, 20, 23, 26,
    31-32, 36, 40, 86-90, 91-97, 100,
    104, 107, 109, 112
Hodgson, Edwin, 11-12; death, 12
Hodgson, Edwina, 12, 20, 23, 26,
    31-32, 36
Hodgson, Eliza Boond, 12, 14-15,
    20, 26; death, 32
Hodgson, Herbert, 12, 13, 15, 16,
    20, 22, 25, 26, 31, 32
Hodgson, John, 12, 13, 15, 16, 20,
    22, 25, 32
Holland, Dr. Josiah, 34
Holmes, Oliver Wendell, Jr., 67
Hutcheson, David, 42

*In Connection with the De Willoughby
    Claim*, 96
In the Closed Room, 80-82
In the Garden, 116
Invalid Children's Aid [Society], 80
Italy, 63, 79, 80, 98, 110

James, Henry, 93
Jordan, Edith. *See* Hodgson, Edith
Jordan, Frank, 90, 103, 109

Kipling, Rudyard, 93
Knoxville, Tennessee, 16, 19-20, 86;
    Frances lives there, 30-38

A Lady of Quality, 87, 88, 91, 97, 111
Lancashire county, England, 11, 34,
    35, 39, 43
Lankester, Dr. Owen, 74
lawsuits: *Fauntleroy*, 63-65; Annie
    Fahnestock's, 112-113
Leslie, Elsie, 66-67
Life Magazine, 119
Little Lord Fauntleroy, 49-54, 61,
    74, 98, 107, 108, 111, 117, 118, 119;
    as a film, 111, 115-116, 119, 121; as

a play, 49, 63-64, 65-66, 111;
clothes, 49, 119; and Vivian,
49-51, 90, 109, 118-119; lawsuit,
63-65, 88; plot, 51-54; success, 49,
54, 55, 63, 67
A Little Princess, as a book, 56, 101;
as a film, 111, 119, 121; as a play,
100, 101
Little Women, 46
London, 62-63, 64, 70-73, 82, 87-88,
93, 97, 100, 103, 107
Long Island, New York, 117. *See also*
Plandome *and* Roslyn
The Lost Prince, 112
Louisiana, 44

MacDonald, George, 36
The Making of a Marchioness, 94-96
Manchester, England, 11, 12, 13,
15-16, 69, 77
Maytham Hall, Rolvenden, Kent,
93-101, 107
The Methods of Lady Walderhurst,
96
"Miss Carruther's Engagement,"
25-27
movies of Frances' works. *See* films
My Robin, 107

New Market, Tennessee, 20-30, 36,
40-41
New York, New York, 35, 36, 44, 67,
90-91, 100-101, 103, 115, 118
New York Journal and Advertiser, 98
New York Telegraph, 92, 111
New York Times, 67-68, 88-89,
91-92, 100, 112-113; obituary, 117
New York World, 88
newspapers and Frances, 66, 67-68,
79, 86, 88-89, 91-92, 98, 100, 111,
112-113; obituary, 117
"Noah's Ark," New Market, 21

O'Brien, Margaret, 119

The One I Knew the Best of All, 85-86

Paris. *See* France
Paris Universal Exposition, 69, 72
Peterson, Charles, 33, 38
Peterson's Ladies' Magazine, 33, 38,
39
Phyllis, 70
Pickford, Mary, 111, 115-116, 119
Plandome, New York, 102, 103-104,
107, 108, 113, 116
"potboiler," defined, 29-30; 40, 113
The Pretty Sister of José, 101
Prissie, 38-40

Robin, 114-115
The Romantick Lady, 118
Roslyn, New York, 117
royalties, defined, 41; 44, 49, 88, 97
royalty, British, 64, 83, 100, 107, 108
rumors. *See* gossip

St. Germain cemetery. *See* France
St. Monica's Home, 80
St. Nicholas, 45, 49
*Sara Crewe, or What Happened at
Miss Minchin's*, 56-59, 63, 100
Schroder, Ricky, 120, 121
Scribner's (publishing company),
35, 40-41, 43, 63, 97
Scribner's Monthly, 33, 34, 39, 85
The Secret Garden, 10, 107, 117,
119-122; as a film, 119, 121; plot,
104-106
Seebohm, E.V., 63-64, 66
"Seth," 35
The Showman's Daughter, 82
The Shuttle, 94, 103
Smith, Jessie Willcox, 81
Society of British Authors, 65
The Story of a Modern Woman, 87
"Surly Tim's Trouble," 34
Stowe, Harriet Beecher, 13
Swampscott, Massachusetts, 85

T. Tembarom, 108, 113
Temple, Shirley, 119
Tennyson, Alfred, Lord, 65
Thackeray, William Makepeace, 21
That Lass o' Lowrie's, 39, 117; as a book, 40-41; as a play, 44
That Man and I, 101
The Thoroughbred Mongrel, 98
Through One Administration, 47
Thwaite, Ann, 48, 98
Tom Sawyer, 42
Townesend, Stephen, 70, 74-76; career in theater, 70-72, 82-83, 88, 91, 97, 100; death, 111-112; Frances' business manager, 72, 88, 97; marriage to Frances ends, 100, 101; letter to Lionel, 76; relationship with Frances, 88, 92, 97, 98-100; weds Frances, 98
Tudor, Tasha, 119
Twain, Mark, 42

Uncle Tom's Cabin, 13

"Vagabondia Castle," Knoxville, 30
Victoria, Queen, 62, 63, 83, 100, 107, 108; Golden Jubilee, 59, 62-63
Victorian Age, defined, 63
Vonnoh, Bessie Potter, 118

Waiting for the Party, 48
Washington, D.C., 40, 48, 66, 69, 72, 73, 74-75, 76, 85, 86, 88, 90, 91, 98; Frances moves there, 41-42; I Street, 43-54; K Street, 55-67; 1770 Massachusetts Avenue, 67-98
"The White People," 80
World War I, 110-111, 112, 113, 114, 115
World's Fair. *See* Paris Universal Exposition

Zangwill, Israel, 87-88

TEXT ACKNOWLEDGMENTS: In this list of sources for the quotes used in this book, the first page number refers to a page in this book; the page numbers in parentheses refer to the pages of the excerpts in the original source.

Excerpts from *Happily Ever After: A Portrait of Frances Hodgson Burnett* by Constance Buel Burnett, New York: Vanguard, 1965, appear as follows: 90 (146-147); 119 (147).

Excerpts from *The One I Knew the Best of All: A Memory of the Mind of a Child* by Frances Hodgson Burnett, New York: Charles Scribner's Sons, 1893, appear as follows: 10 (256 and 209-210); 13 (215); 14 (198); 14-15 (204); 15 (205, 211-212, and 213); 18 (250); 22 (283 and 241); 24 (290, 291, 292, 304, and 305); 24-25 (306); 25 (300 and 312); 25-26 (319); 26 (320, 320, and 322); 26-27 (323-324); 29 (229); 30 (232-233).

Excerpts are reprinted by permission of Charles Scribner's Sons, an imprint of Macmillan Publishing Company from *The Romantick Lady: The Life Story of an Imagination* by Vivian Burnett, 1927, as follows: 20-21 (33); 33 (47 and 52); 34 (54); 42 (81); 46 (75 and 117); 50 (142); 51 (140); 53 (142); 67 (174); 70 (185); 72-73 (186); 76 (211); 77 (212); 80 (212); 82 (221 and 222); 87 (228); 89 (331); 91 (279); 97 (295); 104 (327); 109 (345 and 346).

Excerpts from *The New York Times* appear on the following pages: 68, 88-89, 91-92, 100, 112-113, and 117. Copyright © 1889, 1895, 1898, 1902, 1916, 1924 by the New York Times company. Reprinted by permission.

Excerpts from *The Knoxville News-Sentinel*, November 1949, appear on pages 73 and 84.

Excerpts are reprinted by permission from *Waiting for the Party: The Life of Frances Hodgson Burnett 1849-1924* © Ann Thwaite, 1974, as follows: 22 (33); 36 (44); 40 (48, 51 and 54); 64 (112); 92 (176-177 and 178); 98 (190); 99 (191-192); 101 (214); 111 (234); 113 (239 and 236); 119 (91).

Excerpt from *Life*, "Little Lord Fauntleroy" by Dorothy Kunhardt, 27:71-4+, December 5, 1949, appears on 118.

Excerpts from *Little Lord Fauntleroy* by Frances Hodgson Burnett, New York: Charles Scribner's Sons, 1886, appear as follows: 51 (12); 53 (179); 54 (179 and 180); 61 (44).

Excerpts from *Sara Crewe, or What Happened at Miss Minchin's* by Frances Hodgson Burnett, New York: Charles Scribner's Sons, 1888, appear as follows: 57 (frontispiece); 56 (17); 57 (33); 58 (52-53).

Excerpts from *In the Closed Room* by Frances Hodgson Burnett, New York: McClure, Phillips & Co., 1904, appear as follows: 81 (33); 81-82 (109); 82 (129).

Excerpt from *A Lady of Quality* by Frances Hodgson Burnett, New York: Scribner, 1896, appears as follows: 87 (24-25).

Excerpts from *My Robin* by Frances Hodgson Burnett, New York: Stokes, 1912, appear as follows: 97 (2 and 22).

Excerpts from *The Secret Garden* by Frances Hodgson Burnett, New York: Stokes, 1911, appear as follows: 104-105; 106 (first edition page references not available).

Excerpt from *In the Garden*, by Frances Hodgson Burnett, New York: Medici Society, 1925, appears on 121 (original page reference not available).

Quotes from interview with Penny Deupree appear on pages 45, 65, 77.

ILLUSTRATION ACKNOWLEDGMENTS The photos and illustrations in this text appear courtesy of: pp. 1, 78, 95 (bottom), 102 (bottom), Manhasset Public Library; pp. 2, 30, 42, 73, 84, 89, Library of Congress; pp. 6, 7, 11, 37 (both), 41, 45 (right), 52 (left), 65 (both), 66 (right), 68 (both), 77, 83, 90, 95 (top), 96, 99, 102 (top), 108, 114, 118 (left), 121, courtesy of Penny Deupree; pp. 10, 45 (left), The Mansell Collection; pp. 14, 22, from *The One I Knew the Best of All*, © 1893 by Charles Scribner's Sons; pp. 16, 62, *Illustrated London News*; pp. 23, 27, *Godey's Lady's Book*; p. 28, *Peterson's Magazine*; pp. 34 (both), 47, 71, 118 (right), Independent Picture Service; pp. 43, 110, *The Bookman*; p. 50, *St. Nicholas Magazine*; pp. 52 (right), 53, from *Little Lord Fauntleroy*, © 1886 by Charles Scribner's Sons; pp. 57, 59, from *Sara Crewe, or What Happened at Miss Minchin's*, © 1888 by Charles Scribner's Sons; p. 60, Sophia Smith Collection; p. 66, from *Editha's Burglar*, © 1888 by Jordan Marsh & Co.; p. 81, from *In the Closed Room*, © 1904 by McClure, Phillips & Co.; pp. 115, 120 (bottom), Collectors Bookstore; p. 120 (upper left & right), Hollywood Book & Poster Co. Maps on pages 17 and 31 by Laura Westlund. Front cover photographs by Appel Color Photography and (inset) courtesy of Penny Deupree; back cover photograph courtesy of Manhasset Public Library.